THE GABA BOOK: HOW

Copyright © 2023 by /
badfeelingsgoaway.com

All rights reserved.

No portion of this book may be reproduced in any form without written permission from the publisher or author, except as permitted by U.S. copyright law.

This publication is designed to provide accurate and authoritative information in regard to the subject matter covered. It is sold with the understanding that neither the author nor the publisher is engaged in rendering legal, investment, accounting or other professional services. While the publisher and author have used their best efforts in preparing this book, they make no representations or warranties with respect to the accuracy or completeness of the contents of this book and specifically disclaim any implied warranties of merchantability or fitness for a particular purpose. No warranty may be created or extended by sales representatives or written sales materials. The advice and strategies contained herein may not be suitable for your situation. You should consult with a professional when appropriate. Neither the publisher nor the author shall be liable for any loss of profit or any other commercial damages, including but not limited to special, incidental, consequential, personal, or other damages.

THE GABA BOOK: HOW TO MAXIMIZE YOUR BRAIN'S CALMING POWER NATURALLY

By

Alexander Wright

Table of Contents

Chapter 1: GABA?

Chapter 2: GABA Supplements and GABA in Food

Chapter 3: Sleep

Chapter 4: Gut Health

Chapter 5: Stress

Chapter 6: Diet

Chapter 7: Exercise

Chapter 8: Supplements

CHAPTER 1: GABA?

When all of your brain chemicals are balanced, they help you feel motivated, active, and energetic. Sometimes they help you feel calm and relaxed.

Your brain gets stuck in the "on" state when you don't have enough GABA, though, making you anxious, stressed, and unable to relax. GABA can soak up extra adrenaline and other stress-related chemicals like a sponge.

GABA is so important for being calm and happy that it's been called "nature's Valium."

Here are some of the most common effects of not having enough GABA:

- For no clear reason, you feel scared and have a knot in your stomach.
- You're frequently late because you're too disorganized to make appointments on time.
- You do a lot of things at once, but when the day is over, you don't have much to show for it.
- You worry about new things all the time, even when things are going well.
- You can't calm down, and your thoughts keep you up at night.

What is GABA (gamma-aminobutyric acid)?

GABA is a neurotransmitter, which means it sends messages between nerve cells in your brain. It makes your brain work more slowly by blocking certain messages in your brain and spinal cord. GABA is known to have a calming effect. It is thought to be very important for keeping nerve cells from firing too quickly, which can happen in times of worry, stress, and fear. GABA is also known as a non-protein amino acid.

How Does It Work?

In your brain and spinal cord, GABA is the most common chemical that slows down nerve signals. Inhibitory neurotransmitters stop or block chemical messages and make nerve cells in your brain less stimulated.

Neurotransmitters are chemicals that help nerve cells in your brain talk to each other across the brain. A synapse is a very small space filled with fluid that exists between each nerve cell. This synapse is where neurotransmitters carry their message. They then have to land on and connect to specific receptors on the next nerve cell. This is like a key that can only fit and work in its partner lock.

Nerve cells have two kinds of GABA receptors: GABA-A and GABA-B. Sometimes these receptors work together in different ways, but when GABA binds to them, they make nerve cells less sensitive. So, as an inhibitory neurotransmitter, GABA makes it harder for a nerve cell to get chemical messages from other nerve cells, make chemical messages, or send chemical messages.

What good things does GABA do for your health?

Because it slows down some brain processes, GABA may be able to:

- Reduce stress
- Relieve anxiety
- Improve sleep

What does GABA have to do with glutamate?

Glutamate is like an "on" switch and GABA is like an "off" switch. In your brain, GABA is the main neurotransmitter that stops chemical signals from going from one nerve cell to another. On the other hand, glutamate is the brain's main excitatory receptor. It lets chemical messages get from nerve cell to nerve cell. A careful balance must be kept between the effects of GABA, which slows down brain activity, and glutamate, which speeds up brain activity. Serotonin is another neurotransmitter that works with and through GABA. In fact, many neurotransmitters work with and against each other, and they need to stay in a certain relationship for the brain and body to work right.

GABA is actually made from glutamate. With the help of an enzyme called glutamic acid decarboxylase, glutamate is changed into GABA.

What health problems are linked to changes in the amount of GABA in the body?

When GABA messaging activity ("signaling") isn't balanced and acting as it should, it may be linked to some neurological and mental health conditions. Lessened GABA action may contribute to:

- Anxiety and mood disorders
- Schizophrenia
- Autism
- Depression
- Seizures and epilepsy

Some other health problems linked to GABA dysfunction are:

lack of pyridoxine. In this rare sickness, the body can't make the vitamin that it needs to make GABA. It normally leads to a lot of seizures when the child is young. There is no effective treatment for the seizures with epilepsy drugs, but taking extra vitamins does help

- Hepatic encephalopathy
- Hunting's Disease
- Dystonia and spasticity
- Hypersomnia (being too sleepy during the day or sleeping for too long)

Does raising the amount of GABA in the body have any health benefits?

Researchers are still looking into what happens when GABA levels rise. It's not clear yet, but GABA is being studied to see if it can help treat or avoid health problems like:

- High blood pressure
- Insomnia
- Diabetes
- Anxiety
- Depression

What medicines work on GABA?

The GABA receptors have been used to make a lot of different medicines. Some of these are:

- Benzodiazepines. Some drugs in this group, like diazepam (Valium®) and alprazolam (Xanax®), work on a receptor called GABA-A. Benzodiazepines are used to put people to sleep during surgery, and treat epilepsy, REM sleep problems, alcohol withdrawal, anxiety, essential tremor, and muscle spasticity
- Barbiturates, which are sedatives
- Vigabatrin. This medicine is used to help babies who are having seizures or twitches.
- Flumazenil. This medicine is used to treat benzodiazepine overdose. It is also used to help people with liver encephalopathy feel better mentally
- Valproic Acid. This is a mood-stabilizer and anti-seizure medication.

- Zoolpidem, which is for insomnia.
- Gabapentin, which is for nerve pain and seizures and is prescribed off-label for anxiety, insomnia, restless legs syndrome, and others
- Propfol, which is also a sedative
- Baclofen, which is a muscle relaxer and, like several others on this list, is prescribed off-label for anxiety, insomnia, and more.

Is there a GABA supplement?

GABA can be bought as a food supplement. A lot of it might not be able to get into your brain, though. In the world of science, this is known as "crossing the blood-brain barrier." The barrier is a special membrane that lets only certain chemicals go into and out of your brain. So, no one knows what, if any, effects taking GABA supplements might have on your brain. As of now, there isn't a lot of strong scientific proof that a GABA supplement can help treat health problems. There needs to be more research with more people.

Is there GABA in food?

Some fermented foods, like kimchi, miso, and tempeh, have GABA in them. Green, black, and oolong tea all have it too. Brown rice, soy and adzuki beans, almonds, mushrooms, tomatoes, spinach, broccoli, cabbage, cauliflower, brussels sprouts, sprouted grains, and sweet potatoes are some other foods that contain GABA or help your body make more of it.

Like with supplements, it's not clear if eating things that contain GABA lets GABA get to your brain. There needs to be more research done with more people.

CHAPTER 2: GABA SUPPLEMENTS AND GABA IN FOOD

As for the studies done on GABA supplements, they do provide some encouragement. It seems that GABA tablets may help people who have trouble sleeping. A July 2018 randomized, double-blind clinical trial in the Journal of Clinical Neurology found that GABA supplements (300 milligrams of GABA) made people fall asleep faster and sleep better than a placebo. But this study was very small—only 40 people took part—and bigger studies are needed before any claims can be made.

A February 2018 study published in Brain and Cognition suggests that GABA tablets may help you think and remember things better, in addition to helping you sleep better. This randomized, double-blind, placebo-controlled study found that taking 800 milligrams of GABA as a supplement people smarter and better at paying attention. Before you buy a lot of GABA supplements to help you do better at work or school, though, you should know that this study only had four male subjects.

A study from 2011 in the Journal of Nutritional Science and Vitaminology found that giving a group of 30 healthy people 50 milligrams of GABA as a supplement made them feel less mentally and physically tired. Nine of the people in the group had been diagnosed with chronic fatigue syndrome. Again, this is a small study, and more needs to be done to fully understand how taking GABA supplements can improve health and performance.

Serotonin is a neurotransmitter that is often linked to depression. However, people who are depressed also have low levels of GABA in their cerebrospinal fluid. It looks like taking GABA supplements might help improve your mood, but it looks like no research has been done on using GABA foods or supplements to treat depression.

If you want a more natural way to treat insomnia, anxiety, fatigue, or depression, you should talk to your doctor before adding different supplements to your routine. Even though supplements might not seem dangerous, the FDA says that companies don't have to prove that their goods are safe before they go on sale.

As for food, though it isn't proven that GABA in food can reach the brain, these foods, which some of the highest GABA-containing foods, are also healthy foods that offer a number of other benefits:

- Cruciferous vegetables (broccoli, cabbage, cauliflower, Brussels sprouts)
- Soy beans
- Adzuki beans
- Mushrooms
- Spinach
- Tomatoes
- Buckwheat
- Peas
- Chestnuts
- Sweet potatoes
- Sprouted grains
- Rice (specifically brown rice)
- White tea

It turns out that certain bacterial strains found in your gut, Lactobacillus and Bifidobacterium, produce GABA and may increase the neurotransmitter in your enteric nervous system, which may increase concentration of the neurotransmitter in the cerebrospinal fluid. This means that probiotics may increase GABA. If so, then foods with probiotics in them would be good options for increasing GABA, such as:

- Yogurt. Made from milk fermented by lactic acid bacteria and bifidobacteria, all friendly types of bacteria, yogurt is one of the best sources of probiotics. It's also high in calcium, which is great for your bones.
- Greek yogurt. Also packed with probiotics, Greek yogurt, made by straining regular yogurt, has more protein and few carbs and sugars than other types of yogurt.
- Skyr. This Icelandic dairy product is made by fermenting skim milk and features probiotic cultures similar to yogurt. It's also low in calories and fat and high in protein and other nutrients.
- Sauerkraut. The sour, salty fermented cabbage is probiotic-rich. It's also high in fiber, vitamins and antioxidants but high in sodium.
- Kimchi. A traditional Korean food staple, kimchi is made by fermenting vegetables, including cabbage, with probiotic lactic acid bacteria, and also helps reduce cholesterol, promotes brain health and boosts immunity.
- Tempeh. Because it's high in protein, tempeh is a popular meat substitute. The fermented soybean product is a probiotic food and a good source of vitamin B12.
- Miso. Made by fermenting soybeans with salt and koji, a type of fungus, miso is a Japanese food staple. The paste comes in many varieties and is often used in miso soup. It's also rich in vitamins B, E, K and folic acid.
- Kombucha. A drink made by fermenting black or green tea, sugar, yeast and bacteria, is touted for its

health benefits, including better digestion.
- Kefir. This fermented milk beverage contains multiple strains of friendly bacteria and yeast. It's been shown to improve digestion and has antimicrobial and anti-cancer properties.
- Lassi. A popular drink in India and Pakistan, a lassi is made with fermented yogurt and fruits, like mango, and contains plenty of probiotics.
- Smoothies. Blend your favorite fruits and vegetables with probiotic-rich yogurt for a healthy breakfast or snack that's also protein- and nutrient-dense.
- Turshi. This blend of pickled vegetables, including carrots, celery, peppers, and more, popular in Middle Eastern and Balkan cuisine, contains a wealth of probiotics.
- Pickled onions. Not all pickled onions contain probiotics. To pack more probiotics into your diet, look for ones made using the lacto-fermentation method, where lactic acid bacteria are used in the pickling.
- Pickled beets. When beets are pickled and also fermented, they contain probiotics, along with fiber, vitamins, iron and more.
- Pickled cucumbers. Cucumbers left to ferment in salted water using their natural lactic acid bacteria are rich in probiotics, as well as vitamin K.
- Umeboshi. These Japanese fermented plums are made from unripe ume fruit. Umeboshi may be served whole, in paste form or stored in vinegar.
- Traditional buttermilk. Not to be confused with cultured buttermilk, which is common in the U.S. and is not a probiotic food, traditional buttermilk, made from the liquid leftover after making butter, contains probiotics.
- Sourdough bread. Sourdough depends on wild yeast and lactic acid bacteria, which occur naturally in

- flour, as a leavening agent. And, researchers suggest it may have probiotic-like properties.
- Cottage cheese. Some types of cottage cheese are rich in probiotics, just look for ones that have been fermented with live active cultures.
- Cheddar cheese. Researchers believe the probiotics lactic acid bacteria used as a starter for cheddar cheese could survive the cheese-making and aging processes of cheddar cheese.
- Gouda. Healthy bacteria can survive the cheese-making process for gouda, making it a probiotic-rich cheese.
- Mozzarella. This typical gooey pizza topping is lower in calories and sodium than other cheese, and mozzarella also retains healthy probiotics.
- Feta. This salty sheep's milk cheese is often packed in brine, and researchers think some types of feta have strains of probiotics.
- Provolone. Most cheeses are produced via fermentation, and provolone contains probiotics.
- Parmesan. The hard, aged Italian cheese contains both prebiotic properties and probiotic bacteria, and it's packed with calcium.
- Raw cheeses. The natural bacteria in raw, or unpasteurized, milk can stay alive during cheese-making, as the cheese ferments.
- Sour cream. You probably don't think of sour cream as having many health benefits, but some types contain probiotics.
- Fermented fish. Scientists have found the presence of certain probiotics in a fermented fish, called utonga-kupsu.
- Bananas. Slightly under-ripe bananas are a solid source of prebiotics, which help healthy probiotics grow.
- Garlic. An aromatic and versatile vegetable, garlic is

also a prebiotic food that helps the healthy probiotic bifidobacteria grow in the gut, which could keep diseases away.
- Onions. Rich in fiber and prebiotics, onions can help promote the growth of healthy bacteria in the gut.
- Apple cider vinegar. ACV is touted for its wealth of health benefits. It does contain bacteria, but research is uncertain about its true probiotic effects.
- Balsamic vinegar. Acetic acid is the main compound of balsamic vinegar, and research shows it contains strains of probiotic bacteria, which can improve gut health and the immune system.
- Kvass. Popular in Eastern Europe, kvass is a fermented cereal drink made from malt, rye, flour, stale rye bread and sugar—and, it's a probiotic food.
- Soy sauce. Though it's a fermented food, soy sauce may not always be a probiotic, unless specifically labeled as such. But research suggests it and other fermented foods could also offer gastrointestinal health benefits.
- Olives. Green, kalamata and other kinds of olives, traditionally made via fermentation, often contain lactic acid bacteria.
- Dark chocolate. Research suggests that cocoa can have a similar effect on gut bacteria as probiotics.
- Natto. A popular Japanese breakfast food, natto is a fermented soybean product containing probiotics. Natto is also a good source of protein and vitamin K2, which promotes bone health.
- Cereal. Some cereal brands, including Kellogg's Special K, offer products with probiotics added.
- Apples. Research shows apples contain about 100 million bacteria, which can interact with our gut microbiomes in a healthy way that's more effective than single probiotic supplements.
- Green peas. A Japanese study found that green

peas may contain the probiotic leuconostoc mesenteroides.
- Soy milk. Fermented soy milk may contain probiotics, and other soy milk products may be fortified with probiotics for extra health benefits.
- Dairy alternatives. Many dairy alternatives, such as nut-based milk and yogurt, may contain live cultures. Just check the labels for lactobacillus or other probiotic strains.
- Herbal teas. Already packed with antioxidants, some herbal teas are enriched with probiotics for an extra health boost.
- Celery juice. Research shows celery juice could offer health benefits as a probiotic drink, when enriched with healthy bacteria.
- Bottled probiotic drinks. An easy way to get a probiotic boost is to pick up one of the several probiotic drinks out there, like juices, teas, kombucha and smoothies.
- Beer.Belgian-style beers, such as Hoegaarden and Westmalle Tripel, which are fermented twice, may contain a specific kind of probiotic yeast that can kill harmful bacteria in the gut.
- Microalgae. It often comes in powder form, and microalgae has a number of health benefits and is a good source of probiotics.
- Spirulina. A type of blue-green algae, spirulina is a popular supplement that's full of nutrients, including probiotics.
- Supplements. Most nutrition experts say the best probiotic sources come directly from foods, but there are plenty of probiotic supplements, too. The Cleveland Clinic recommends probiotic products with "1 billion colony forming units" at least and the probiotics lactobacillus or bifidobacterium.

CHAPTER 3: SLEEP

The quality, duration, and consistency of your sleep effects every aspect of your health, including your mental health, with severe implications for your anxiety. Poor sleep is associated with low GABA levels and excess glutamate levels, resulting in stress, anxiety, depression, and more.

How Much Sleep Do We Need?
The amount of sleep differs based, first, on age. The general recommendations according to The National Center for Biotechnology Information are:

Age Group	Age Range	Recommended
Infant	4-12 months	12-16 hours
Toddler	1-2 years	11-14 hours
Preschool	3-5 years	0-13 hours
School-age	6-12 years	9-12 hours
Teen	13-18 years	8-10 hours
Adult	18 years and older	7-9 hours

This table does not include recommendations for newborns because their needs vary wildly, ranging anywhere from 11 hours to 19 hours per 24-hour period.

The American Academy of Sleep Medicine put together a group of experts on sleep to come up with these suggestions. The group members looked at hundreds of high-quality studies about the link between how long you sleep and important health issues like heart disease, depression, pain, and diabetes.

After looking at the facts, the group went through several rounds of voting and talking to narrow down the numbers for how much sleep different ages need. Other medical groups, like the Sleep Research Society, the American Academy of Pediatrics, and more, have agreed with the final suggestions.

It is essential to understand that these are general recommendations. You are an individual. As an individual, your needs may be different than others. Here are some things to consider that may have an impact on your individual needs. To figure out how much sleep you need, you must think about your overall health, the things you do every day, and how you usually sleep. Some things that can help you figure out how much sleep you need are:

- Do you feel healthy, happy, and active after seven hours of sleep? Or, have you found that you need more sleep to really get going?
- Do you have more than one health problem that might need you to rest more?
- Do you use a lot of energy every single day? Do you play sports or have a job that requires a lot of physical work?
- Do the things you do every day require you to be alert to do them safely? Do you drive a lot every day or use big equipment? Do any of these things ever make you feel sleepy?
- Do you have trouble sleeping or have you had trouble sleeping in the past?
- Does caffeine help you get through the day?
- Do you tend to sleep in more when you have a lot of free time?

You can figure out how much sleep you need based on how you answer these questions.

Sleeping Too Much

While individual concerns are relevant, there is a limit. Most people know that getting too little sleep can hurt your health. Getting too little sleep on a regular basis is linked to several long-term diseases, as well as making you cranky and tired during the day. But did you know that sleeping too much can also be bad? Oversleeping is linked to several health issues, as well such as:

- Type 2 diabetes
- Heart trouble
- Obesity
- Depression
- Headaches

Does sleeping too much make you sick, or is it a sign of a problem you already have? Either way, you might want to see your doctor if you are always falling asleep or looking for the next nap.

If you need more than 8 or 9 hours of sleep every night to feel relaxed, this could be a sign of a deeper problem. Many things affect the quality of your sleep, making you feel tired and sluggish even after 8 hours in bed. Among these problems are:

- Sleep apnea
- Restless legs syndrome
- Bruxism (teeth grinding)
- Chronic pain
- Some prescription drugs

Then there are situations that don't change the quality of your sleep much but make you need more sleep. Among them are:

- Narcolepsy
- Delayed sleep phase syndrome
- Idiopathic hypersomnia

These problems can be treated, which can help you sleep better.

Many people think it's a normal part of aging that they need more sleep, but getting older shouldn't make a big difference in how much sleep you need.

If you've checked out those problems and you're still hitting the snooze button after 9 hours under the covers, it could be a sign that you have a heart problem, diabetes, or depression, and you should speak to a doctor. He or she might also suggest a sleep study to make sure there aren't any sleep problems.

Sleeping Too Little

Simply not getting enough sleep is referred to as sleep deprivation, but there is a broader concept known as "sleep deficiency," which encompasses sleep deprivation as well as other issues. Sleep deficiency can be caused by any of the following:

- You don't get enough sleep.
- You sleep at the wrong time of day.
- You don't sleep well or get all the different kinds of sleep your body needs.
- You have a sleep disorder that makes it hard for you to get enough sleep or makes the sleep you do get less restful.

People need to sleep just as much as they need to eat, drink, and breathe and is just as important to your health and happiness as these other things. About one-third of people in the United States don't get enough rest or sleep every day, according to the Centers for Disease Control and Prevention. Nearly 40% of people say they fall asleep during the day at least once a month when they didn't mean to. Also, between 50 and 70 million Americans have sleep problems that don't go away. Lack of sleep can cause problems with your physical and mental health, accidents, less work output, and even a higher chance of dying. Lack of sleep can make it hard to do well at your job, school, driving, and with other people. You might find it hard to learn, pay attention, and move. Also, it might be hard for you to understand how other people feel and act. Lack of sleep can also make you feel angry, irritable, or worried around other people.

Children and adults may have different signs of not getting enough sleep. When kids don't get enough sleep, they might be overly active and have trouble paying attention. They might also misbehave, which can hurt how well they do in school.

Adults, teens, and kids who don't get enough sleep are also more likely to get hurt. For example, sleepiness while driving is a major cause of serious injuries and deaths in car accidents. When it comes to older people, not getting enough sleep may make them more likely to fall and break a bone. People who don't get enough sleep have also made mistakes that led to terrible accidents like nuclear plant meltdowns, big ships running aground, and plane crashes.

People often believe that they can get by with less sleep and nothing bad will happen. But studies show that getting enough good sleep at the right times is important for mental health, physical health, quality of life, and safety.

Science of Sleep

There are many things that help your body get ready to sleep and wake up. Your body has several internal clocks called circadian clocks. These typically follow a 24-hour repeating rhythm called the circadian rhythm. This rhythm affects every cell, tissue, and organ in your body.

Your central circadian clock, located in your brain, tells you when it is time for sleep. Other circadian clocks are in organs throughout your body. Your body's internal clocks are in sync with certain cues in the environment. Light, darkness, and other cues help determine when you feel awake and when you feel drowsy. Artificial light and caffeine can disrupt this process by giving your body false wakefulness cues.

Your body clock may not be the same as other people's. The natural circadian cycle of most people is a little longer than 24 hours. Some people wake up early by nature, while others stay up late by nature. For example, it's normal for many teenagers to want to go to bed later and wake up later.

With age, the rhythm and timing of body clocks also change. Neurons, or cells, that help you sleep are lost as a normal part of getting older. Some diseases, like Alzheimer's, can also speed up the death of neurons. This makes it harder for older people to sleep through the night. Circadian rhythms can also be changed by things like less physical activity or less time spent outside. Because of this, most older people sleep less and wake up earlier.

When you have been awake for a long time, your body's biological need for sleep grows. This is controlled by homeostasis, the process by which your body keeps your systems, like your internal body temperature, stable. This need to sleep is linked to a chemical called adenosine. The amount of adenosine in your brain keeps going up as long as you are awake. The shift toward sleep is shown by the rising levels. This process can be stopped by caffeine and other drugs that block adenosine.

If you follow the natural pattern of days and nights, your eyes send signals to your brain that it is daytime. The part of your brain that gets these signals is called the suprachiasmatic nucleus. The sympathetic system and the parasympathetic system send these signals to the rest of your body. This helps your body's main clock keep track of day and night. This process is messed up when people are exposed to artificial light.

The cycle of light and dark affects when your brain makes and releases melatonin. Your bloodstream carries melatonin to the cells in your body. Melatonin starts to build up in your bloodstream in the evening and reaches its highest level in the early morning. Melatonin is thought to help you fall asleep. When you're exposed to more light, like when the sun comes up, your body makes a chemical called cortisol. Cortisol helps your body get ready to wake up on its own.

If you are exposed to bright artificial light late at night, it can mess up this process and stop your brain from making melatonin. This can make it more difficult to go to sleep. Bright artificial light comes from things like a TV screen, a smartphone, or an alarm clock with a very bright light. Some people use physical filters or software to block some of the blue light from these devices.

Your central circadian clock is not always in sync with the time you go to sleep. Jet lag or night shifts can cause it to go out of sync.

When you sleep, you go back and forth between two stages: rapid eye movement (REM) sleep and non-REM sleep. Every 80 to 100 minutes, the cycle starts again. Most nights, there are four to six cycles. Between cycles, you might wake up for a short time.

Non-REM sleep has three stages:

Stage 1: This is the transition between being awake and going to sleep.

Stage 2: At this point, you are asleep.

Stage 3. This stage of sleep is called deep sleep or slow-wave sleep. You usually spend more time in this stage earlier in the night.

REM sleep is when your eyes twitch and your brain is active. Brain activity during REM sleep is about the same as brain activity when you are awake. REM sleep is when most people dream. Most of the time, your muscles weaken, preventing you from acting out your dreams. You typically have more REM sleep later in the night, but you don't get as much REM sleep in colder temperatures. This is because your body doesn't regulate your temperature properly during REM sleep.

As people get older, their sleep habits and types change. For example, babies spend more time in REM sleep. The amount of slow-wave sleep is highest when a child is young and drops sharply when he or she is a teenager. Slow-wave sleep gets less and less as people get older, and some older people may not have any at all.

The way you feel while you are awake depends in part on

what happens while you are sleeping. During sleep, your body is working to support healthy brain function and maintain your physical health.

Children and teens also grow and develop better when they get enough sleep. It can also affect how well you think, act, work, learn, and get along with others.

When you fall asleep and go into non-REM sleep, your heart rate and blood pressure drop. During sleep, your body is controlled by your parasympathetic system, and your heart doesn't have to work as hard as it does when you're awake. Your sympathetic nervous system is turned on during REM sleep and when you wake up. This raises your heart rate and blood pressure to your usual levels when awake and calm.

People who don't get enough sleep or wake up often at night may be more likely to have:

- Coronary artery disease
- High blood pressure
- Obesity
- Stroke

At different times of the day, your body makes different hormones. This may be related to your sleep patterns or circadian clocks. Your body makes hormones, like cortisol, that make you more awake in the morning. Other hormones have 24-hour cycles that change as you age. For example, in children, the hormones that tell the glands to release testosterone, estrogen, and progesterone are made in pulses at night, and the pulses get bigger as puberty approaches.

Different circadian clocks, such as those in the liver, fat, and muscle, affect how your body deals with fat. For example, these circadian clocks make sure that your liver is ready to help digest fat at the right times. If you eat at odd times, your body may handle fat in a different way.

Studies have shown that not getting enough good sleep can

lead to:

- Higher levels of hunger-controlling hormones like leptin and ghrelin in your body.
- Less ability to respond to insulin.
- More eating, especially fatty, sweet, and salty foods.
- Decreased physical activity
- Metabolic Syndrome

And all these things can contribute to being overweight or obese.

During sleep, you take in less oxygen and breathe less often and less deeply. People with health problems like asthma or chronic obstructive pulmonary disease (COPD) may have trouble with these changes. Most of the time, asthma symptoms are worse in the early morning. People with lung diseases like COPD can also have trouble breathing that gets worse at night.

Sleep also affects your immune system. Different parts of your immune system are more active at different times of the day. For example, a certain type of immune cell works harder when you sleep. Because of this, people who don't get enough sleep may get colds and other infections more often.

Sleep helps with learning and the formation of long-term memories. If you don't get enough sleep or high-quality sleep, it can be more difficult to concentrate on tasks and think clearly.

Sleep Hygiene

Sleep hygiene may be the most talked about subject when it comes to sleep. Your sleep hygiene can make a pivotal difference to your sleep. Here are some of the most common and most effective do's and don't of sleep hygiene.

What to do:

- Try to sleep around the same time each night and wake up

around the same time each morning.

- Exercise for at least 30 minutes a day, about five days a week. Exercise hard only in the morning or afternoon. Before bed, you can do more relaxing exercises, like yoga.
- Get a lot of sunlight. Open your blinds as soon as you wake up and spend some time outside at some point. You can also use a light box first thing in the morning on dark winter days to help your brain wake up and keep your body's rhythms in sync.
- Set up a regular, relaxing routine for going to bed.
- Take a warm shower or bath before you go to sleep.
- Do relaxation exercises like mindful breathing and progressive muscle relaxation before you go to sleep.
- Make sure the place where you sleep is nice and calm. Your room shouldn't be too hot, too cold, or too bright, and your bed should be comfortable. Use earplugs and an eye mask if you feel the need. Make sure your pillow feels good.
- Reserve your bed for sleep and sex. Don't eat, watch TV, or work in bed.
- Go to bed when you're tired and get out of bed if you can't sleep.
- Don't have a clock within sight.
- Turn off your phone's alerts for texts and emails.
- Write down your worries in a "worry journal." If you can't sleep because you're thinking about something, write it down so you can think about it again the next day.
- If you can't fall asleep after about 20 minutes, get out of bed, and do something relaxing, like reading. When you're ready to sleep again, go back to bed.
- If you want to use your computer late at night, you can get free software for your computer that lets you dim the screen. f.lux and Dimmer are two well-known programs. Even better, turn off the computer an hour before bed.

What to avoid:
- Don't ingest caffeine after noon. This includes soda, coffee, tea, iced tea, and energy drinks.
- Don't drink too much alcohol at night. Alcohol is known to make it easier to fall asleep, but it also makes it harder to stay asleep. This is especially true in the second half of the night, when the body should be going into deep sleep.
- Don't take other stimulants like chocolate, nicotine, or some medicines close to bedtime.
- Don't eat a big meal right before bed.
- Before bed, don't watch TV, use the computer, or spend a long time on your phone. These things make your brain work, which makes it harder to fall asleep.
- Don't use your phone, laptop, or any other mobile device in bed.
- Don't give in to the urge to take a nap in the middle of the day. It can throw off your normal sleep-wake cycle.

It's essential to note, once again, that you are an individual. You don't necessarily need to follow everything on this list. Some people watch television before bed, and it helps them relax and improves their mood, thus improving their sleep. These recommendations are based on technicalities. Technically, the exposure to the light of the television and the stimulation of what's on screen should have a negative impact on sleep, but if the benefits for you outweigh this minor impact, then sleep can be improved. This applies to almost everything on the list. These should be thought of more as suggestions. Give them a chance and see if they work for you. If something doesn't help or seems to make it worse, stop that. As an extreme example, if drinking a cup of coffee right before bed somehow, paradoxically, helped you sleep, then the fact that nearly everyone on the planet would recommend otherwise is not relevant. Do what works for you. The preceding list is simply a list of methods that have been tested for decades and have been found to work for countless people. They may work for you. They may not.

Histamine

Histamine controls many body functions and is a key part of your body's response to inflammation. Which histamine receptors histamine binds to determines what effect it has. Scientists have found four different kinds of histamine receptors. Excess histamine can cause anxiety as well as insomnia.

H1 receptors

You have H1 receptors all over your body, including in neurons (brain cells), smooth muscle cells in your airways, and blood vessels. When the H1 receptors are turned on, allergy and anaphylaxis symptoms show up. It can lead to:

- Itchy skin (pruritus)
- Anxiety
- Expanding of blood vessels (vasodilation)
- Hypotension (low blood pressure)
- Increased heart rate (tachycardia)
- Flushing
- Narrowing of your airway (bronchoconstriction)
- Pain
- Movement of fluids through blood vessel walls (vascular permeability)

Some of these changes in the body cause sneezing, stuffy nose, and a runny nose (rhinorrhea).

H1 receptors do more than just control allergic reactions. They also help:

- Sleep-wake cycles
- Food intake

- Body temperature
- Emotions
- Memory
- Learning

Of course, its effect on sleep-wake cycles is our current concern.

Histamine is considered wake-promoting because drowsiness is a common side effect of certain anti-allergy medications that block histamine signaling. Also, histamine neurons are generally active in wake states and inactive during sleep. Histamine neurons promote wakefulness by activating neurons in the cortex that cause arousal and by inhibiting neurons that promote sleep. So, basically, histamine keeps you awake.

How to Reduce Histamine Naturally

Foods that reduce histamine:

- Apples
- Onions
- Pineapple
- Parsley
- Blueberries
- Olive oil

Vitamin C reduces histamines, as well, so any foods containing vitamin C may reduce histamine.

Foods to avoid if you trying to reduce histamine:

- Kombucha
- Sauerkraut
- Wine or beer
- Aged meats or cheese
- Olives
- Vinegar

- Canned meats/fish
- Tomatoes
- Ketchup
- Avocados
- Spinach

Supplements that may help reduce histamine:

- Forskolin
- Quercetin
- Astragalus
- Vitamin C
- B. longum (probiotic strain)
- B. infantis (probiotic strain)
- Erythropoietin
- Pancreatic enzymes (ask a doctor before use)
- Methylxanthines (Dietary sources of methylxanthines include coffee, tea, chocolate, maté, and guarana. You can drink coffee, eat chocolate, or supplement with theobromine, but attempting to supplement with theophylline is not recommended, as adverse cardiac effects are possible. However, chocolate also contains some histamine, and researchers suspect that it may encourage histamine release. The net effect of cocoa is unknown; it's recommended that you test your own individual response and see what it does for you.)
- Fisetin
- Luteolin (found in celery, parsley, and broccoli)
- Apigenin (found in parsley, grapes, and apples)
- EGCG (found in green tea)
- Kaempferol (found in cruciferous vegetables, delphinium plants, witch hazel, and grapefruit)
- Myricetin (found in berries, teas, wines, and many vegetables)
- Rutin (found in buckwheat, apples, and passionflower)
- Theanine (found in green and black tea)

- Naringenin (found in grapefruit)
- Curcumin (found in turmeric)
- Reishi mushroom
- Chinese Skullcap
- Eleuthero (also known as Siberian ginseng)
- Tulsi (also known as holy basil)
- Mucuna pruriens (also known as velvet bean)
- Vitamin B6
- L. plantarum (a probiotic)
- Palmitoylethanolamide (PEA)
- SAM-e (S-adenosyl-L-methionine)
- Carnosine (made from the amino acids beta-alanine and histidine and found in high-quality meat)
- NAC (N-acetyl cysteine)
- Valine (found in meat, grains, vegetables, and milk and other dairy products)

Drugs that reduce histamine:
- alimemazine (trimeprazine)
- brompheniramine
- chlorphenamine
- dexchlorpheniramine
- diphenhydramine (Benadryl)
- doxylamine (often sold under the brand name "Unisom," though Unisom sometimes contains diphenhydramine instead)
- pheniramine
- promethazine
- triprolidine
- hydroxyzine

These should be reserved for occasional, short-term use only. You can quickly develop tolerance to them, and side-effects may occur with prolonged use.

Cortisol

Cortisol is a steroid hormone that is made and released by your adrenal glands. These glands are endocrine glands that sit on top of your kidneys. Cortisol affects many parts of your body, but its main job is to control how your body reacts to stress. Cortisol is a hormone called a glucocorticoid that is made and released by your adrenal glands.

Glucocorticoids are a kind of hormone called a steroid. They stop inflammation in your body's tissues and keep your muscles, fat, liver, and bones from breaking down too quickly. Glucocorticoids also change the way people sleep and wake up.

Your body checks your cortisol levels all the time to keep them steady (this is called homeostasis). Cortisol levels that are either too high or too low can be bad for your health.

People often call cortisol the "stress hormone." But it does a lot more than just control your body's stress response. It has many important effects and functions all over your body. Also, it's important to keep in mind that, from a biological point of view, there are many kinds of stress, such as:

- Acute stress: This kind of stress happens when you are suddenly and for a short time in danger. Acute stress can be caused by things like barely avoiding a car accident or being chased by an animal.
- Chronic stress: This is long-term stress that happens when you must deal with things that make you angry or worried over and over again. Chronic stress can be caused by things like having a job that is hard or frustrating or being sick all the time.
- Traumatic stress: This happens when you go through something that puts your life in danger and makes you feel scared and helpless. Traumatic stress can be caused by things like being in a war or being sexually assaulted or

going through a tornado. Post-traumatic stress disorder (PTSD) can sometimes be caused by these things.

When any of these things stress you out, your body makes cortisol.

How does my body react to cortisol?

When you're stressed, your body can release cortisol after releasing "fight or flight" hormones like adrenaline. This keeps you on high alert. In times of stress, cortisol also makes your liver release glucose (sugar) so that you can get energy quickly. Cortisol helps control how your body uses fats, proteins, and carbs for energy by regulating your metabolism.

Normally, your cortisol levels are lowest in the evening when you go to sleep and highest in the morning before you wake up. This suggests that cortisol is a key part of waking up and is involved in the circadian rhythm of your body. Cortisol levels need to be just right for people to live and for their bodies to work properly. If your cortisol levels are consistently high or low, it can be bad for your health. High cortisol levels can cause anxiety.

How does my body keep the level of cortisol in check?

Your body has a complicated system to control how much cortisol you have in your body. Your hypothalamus, which is a small part of your brain that controls hormones, and your pituitary gland, which is a small gland below your brain, controls how much cortisol your adrenal glands make. When the amount of cortisol in your blood drops, your hypothalamus releases corticotropin-releasing hormone (CRH), which tells your pituitary gland to make adrenocorticotropic hormone (ACTH). Then, ACTH tells your adrenal glands to make cortisol and let it out. Your hypothalamus, pituitary gland, and adrenal glands must all be working well for you to have the right amount of cortisol in your body.

How can I find out how much cortisol I have?

Your doctor can test your blood, urine, or saliva to see how much cortisol is in your body. Based on your symptoms, they will decide which test is best.

How much cortisol is normal?

Cortisol is a hormone that is found in your blood, urine, and saliva. Its level is highest in the morning and drops throughout the day, reaching its lowest point around midnight. If you work nights and sleep at different times, this pattern can change.

The normal ranges for most tests that measure cortisol in your blood are:

- 10 to 20 micrograms per deciliter (mcg/dL) from 6 to 8 a.m.
- 3 to 10 mcg/dL around 4 p.m.

Normal ranges can be different from lab to lab, person to person, and over time. If you need a cortisol level test, your doctor or nurse will look at the results and tell you if you need more testing.

What makes cortisol levels so high?

Hypercortisolism is the medical term for having abnormally high levels of cortisol for a long time. This is usually considered Cushing's Syndrome, which is a rare condition. Causes of cortisol levels that are higher than normal and Cushing's Syndrome include:

- Taking a lot of corticosteroid drugs like prednisone, prednisolone, or dexamethasone to treat other health problems.

- Tumors that produce adrenocorticotropic hormone (ACTH). These are usually found in your pituitary gland. More rarely, neuroendocrine tumors in other parts of your body such as your lungs can cause high cortisol levels.
- Adrenal gland tumors or excessive growth of adrenal tissue (hyperplasia), which cause excess production of cortisol.

What are the signs that your cortisol levels are too high?

Depending on how high your cortisol levels are, your symptoms of Cushing's Syndrome will be different. Common signs and symptoms of cortisol levels that are higher than normal are:

- Weight gain, especially in your face and abdomen.
- Anxiety
- Fatty deposits between your shoulder blades.
- Wide, purple stretch marks on your abdomen (belly).
- Muscle weakness in your upper arms and thighs.
- High blood sugar, which often turns into Type 2 diabetes.
- High blood pressure (hypertension).
- Excessive hair growth (hirsutism) in women.
- Weak bones (osteoporosis) and fractures.
-

What causes cortisol to be low?

When cortisol levels are lower than normal, this is called hypocortisolism. This is a sign of adrenal insufficiency. There are two kinds of adrenal insufficiency: primary and secondary. Some things that can cause adrenal insufficiency are:

- Primary adrenal insufficiency: Most of the time, your immune system attacks healthy cells in your adrenal glands for no known reason, which can cause primary adrenal insufficiency. The name for this is Addison's disease. Your adrenal glands can also be hurt by an infection or bleeding in the tissues (called an adrenal hemorrhage). All these things stop cortisol from being made.

- Secondary adrenal insufficiency: If you have hypopituitarism or a tumor on your pituitary gland, it can stop your body from making enough ACTH. ACTH tells your adrenal glands to make cortisol, so when there isn't enough ACTH, there isn't enough cortisol made.

Corticosteroid medications can also cause cortisol levels to be lower than normal, especially if you stop taking them quickly after using them for a long time.

What are the signs that your cortisol levels are too low?

If your cortisol levels are lower than normal, this is called adrenal insufficiency.

- Fatigue
- Anxiety
- Unintentional weight loss
- Poor appetite
- Hypotension (low blood pressure)

How can I lower my level of cortisol?

If you have Cushing's syndrome, which is when your cortisol levels are very high, you will need medical treatment to bring them down. Most treatments involve either medicine or surgery. If your cortisol levels are lower than normal, you'll also need medical help.

In general, though, there are a few simple things you can do every day to try to lower your cortisol levels and keep them where they should be.

- Get good sleep: Sleep problems like obstructive sleep

- apnea, insomnia, or working the night shift can cause cortisol levels to rise.
- Regular exercise: Several studies have shown that regular exercise can help you sleep better and feel less stressed, which can lower your cortisol levels over time.
- Learn to control stress and stressful ways of thinking: Knowing how you think, how you breathe, how fast your heart beats, and other signs of stress can help you catch it early and stop it from getting worse.
- Do exercises that help you take deep breaths: Your parasympathetic nervous system, or "rest and digest" system, is activated when you breathe in a controlled way. This helps lower cortisol levels.
- Have fun and laugh: Laughing makes endorphins come out and stops cortisol from coming out. Having hobbies and doing fun things can also make you feel better, which may make your cortisol levels go down.
- Keep your relationships in good shape: Relationships are an important part of our life. Having tense, unhealthy relationships with people you care about or work with can cause you to feel stressed out often and raise your cortisol levels.

When should I talk to my doctor about my cortisol levels?

If you have signs of Cushing's syndrome or adrenal insufficiency, you should see a doctor. If you are worried about how stressed you are every day, talk to your doctor or nurse about what you can do to reduce your stress and stay healthy.

Cortisol is a very important hormone that affects a lot of different parts of your body. There are a few things you can do to try to reduce your stress and, by extension, your cortisol levels. However, sometimes you can't help whether your cortisol levels are too high or too low. If you gain or lose weight, or if your blood pressure goes up or down, these are signs that your cortisol levels are too high or too low. You should talk to your doctor about this. They can do some simple tests to find out if your symptoms are caused by your adrenal glands or your pituitary gland.

Foods that lower cortisol:
- Avocados
- Bananas
- Broccoli
- Dark Chocolate
- Seeds
- Spinach
- Nutritional yeast
- Probiotics
- Olive Oil
- Nuts
- Adaptogens such as mushrooms, moringa and ashwagandha
- Cinnamon

Supplements that lower cortisol:
- Ashwagandha
- Omega-3s
- Prebiotics
- Probiotics
- Rhodiola Rosea
- Bacopa Monnieri
- Ginkgo Biloba
- Cordyceps
- Phosphatidylserine
- L-theanine

Norepinephrine

Norepinephrine is a neurotransmitter and a hormone. It is

also called noradrenaline. It is a key part of the "fight-or-flight" response in your body. Norepinephrine is also a drug that is used to raise and keep blood pressure high in short-term, serious health situations. As a neurotransmitter, norepinephrine is made from dopamine. Norepinephrine is made by nerve cells in your brainstem and in an area close to your spinal cord. Norepinephrine is a part of your body's sympathetic nervous system, which is part of your "fight-or-flight" response to danger. The "fight or flight" response is called the "acute stress response" in medicine. If you have too much norepinephrine, you may feel anxious or on edge.

How does the body use norepinephrine?
- It makes you more awake, alert, and focused.
- Blood vessels get smaller, which helps keep blood pressure steady when you're stressed.
- Changes the way you sleep, how you feel, and what you remember.

What sets off the release of norepinephrine?

Norepinephrine is a hormone that comes out of your adrenal glands when you're stressed. The fight-or-flight response is the name for the changes in your body that happen because of this response.

What does "fight or flight" mean?

The fight-or-flight response is how your body reacts to stressful situations, like when you need to get away from a dangerous situation (like a dog that is growling) or when you have to face a fear (like giving a speech for school or work). During the fight-or-flight response, your brain tells you that something bad is happening. Then, nerves in a part of your brain called the hypothalamus send a message down your spinal cord and out to the rest of your body. Norepinephrine is the neurotransmitter that tells your nervous system what to do when your brain tells it what to do. The neurotransmitter noradrenaline goes to these organs and tissues and causes these quick reactions in the body:

- Eyes: The pupils get bigger to let in more light so you can see more of what's around you.
- Skin: Your skin goes pale when your blood vessels get a message to send blood to places that need it more, like your muscles, so you can fight or run away.
- Heart: The heart beats harder and faster to get more oxygenated blood to places like your muscles that need it most. Also, blood pressure goes up.
- Muscles: When muscles get more blood flow and oxygen, they can move and work faster and with more strength.
- Liver: Your liver turns the glycogen you have stored into glucose, which gives you more energy.
- Airways: People breathe faster and deeper. Your airways widen, which lets more oxygen into your blood, which then goes to your muscles.

Your adrenal gland releases the hormones adrenaline (epinephrine) and noradrenaline (norepinephrine) when the neurotransmitter noradrenaline gets to it. These hormones get to every part of your body through your blood. They go back to your eyes, heart, lungs, skin, blood vessels, and adrenal gland. The "message" to these organs and tissues is to keep reacting until the danger is gone.

Norepinephrine is used as a medicine to raise and keep blood pressure up in situations where low blood pressure is a problem, but only for a short time. Some of these conditions could be:

- Cardiac arrest
- Spinal anesthesia
- Septicemia
- Blood transfusions

- Drug reactions

Low levels of norepinephrine can cause the following health problems:
- Anxiety
- Depression
- ADHD
- Headache
- Memory problems
- Sleeping problems
- Hypotension (low blood pressure)
- Low blood sugar (hypoglycemia)
- Blood pressure and heart rate changes
- Dopamine beta-hydroxylase deficiency. Your body can't turn dopamine into norepinephrine if you have this rare genetic disease

High levels of epinephrine can cause the following health problems:
- High blood pressure
- Rapid or irregular heartbeat
- Excessive sweating
- Pale or cold skin
- Frequent headaches
- Nervous feeling, jitters
- Pheochromocytoma, which is a growth on the adrenal glands

People with high levels of norepinephrine are more likely to hurt their heart, blood vessels, or kidneys. To lower norepinephrine, it's important to find ways to put your body into parasympathetic response mode, so anything in nature that can help you relax will do. Norepinephrine levels can be kept in check by eating a well-balanced diet, reducing emotional and physical stress, getting enough sleep, and exercising regularly.

- Nutrition

A well-balanced diet has been shown to help keep your immune system healthy and give you the extra energy you need to deal with stress. Early research suggests that omega-3 fatty acids and vegetables may help control cortisol levels. Mindful eating reduces stress by encouraging people to take deep breaths, choose their food carefully, pay attention to the meal, and chew their food slowly and thoroughly. This can also help your body digest better.

- Herbs and Supplements

Calming amino acids like a theanine supplement can help support norepinephrine levels, and nervine botanicals like lemon balm, kava, and chamomile, which work on the nervous system, can help naturally lower norepinephrine levels.

There has been a lot of research on how adaptogenic herbs like ashwagandha can help the nervous system adapt to stressors, which can reduce stress and anxiety in people who use them regularly.

Melatonin has been shown to lower the amount of norepinephrine in the body because it helps the sympathetic tone.

- Lifestyle

Physical activity can help lower stress hormones and blood pressure. Aerobic exercise raises your heart rate and breathing rate, which lets more oxygen flow through your body.

Meditation, yoga, and tai chi all focus on deep breathing, which can help the parasympathetic nervous system help fight stress.

Some research shows that using cognitive behavioral therapy (CBT) can help lower norepinephrine levels, which are often high in people who are anxious or angry.

Supplements

Many supplements are known to assist sleep. Here are some of the better known and more widely used and studied ones available.

- Lavender

Lavender oil seems to have a soothing effect and reduces anxiety and restlessness. Most studies on lavender's efficacy as a sleep aid have focused on lavender essential oil, though some people also use the dried herb as a tea or in their pillow. Essential oils should not be ingested except under a doctor's supervision, as even lavender oil contains poisonous compounds. Instead, the oil should be diffused into the air or diluted in a neutral cream or oil for use on the skin.

Lavender may be most appealing for people who struggle to sleep due to anxiety or racing thoughts. It is also popular among people who want an external sleep aid rather than something they consume. Short-term use of dried lavender or use of lavender essential oil is thought to be safe, though potential side effects for the external use of lavender oil include skin irritation and allergic reaction.

Lavendar is also available as a clinically-studied supplement called Lavela WS 1265.

- Valerian

Valerian has been used for sleep problems since the 2nd century. Though further research needs to be done, valerian appears to help people fall asleep faster, sleep better, and wake up less often. In some studies, patients taking valerian were 80%

more likely to report sleep improvements than those taking a placebo.

Because experts have not located a single active compound, they speculate that valerian's effect may be due to several compounds working together, or the amino acids GABA or glycine.

The roots and stems of the valerian plant are made into teas, tinctures, capsules, extracts, and tablets. While each type of preparation has its fans, the tea can have an unpleasant odor, and researchers generally use liquid extracts or capsules in their research. Valerian is usually recommended for people with insomnia or general problems with sleep quality. Most people report that it is more effective once they have been taking it for several weeks. However, further research is needed to determine how effective valerian is in treating insomnia.

Valerian is generally considered safe for adults. Side effects are rare and tend to be mild but may include headache, dizziness, itching, and upset stomach.

- German Chamomile

German chamomile has been used to treat sleep problems since ancient Egypt. Despite this long history, there has been little research into its benefits. What we do know from smaller studies and meta-analysis is that German chamomile may soothe anxiety and improve sleep quality, although researchers are not clear on why it might have these effects. On the other hand, it does not appear to benefit people with insomnia.

The most common preparations of German chamomile are capsules, tincture, and tea. Although there is another variety called Roman chamomile, most research has focused on the German type.

Chamomile is generally regarded as safe when used as a tea or taken orally. It does have potential interactions with some drugs, including blood thinners, and there is little information on its safety for those who are pregnant or breastfeeding. Side effects are usually limited to mild nausea or dizziness, but allergic reactions are possible, particularly for people with allergies to related plants like ragweed and daisies.

- Passionflower

The passionflower vine is native to the Americas and has historically been used as a sedative by multiple indigenous cultures. There has been very little research into its benefits, though the existing research is encouraging, if limited. In one study focused on generalized anxiety disorder, passionflower's calming effects were comparable to a commonly prescribed sedative. Passionflower may also improve sleep quality and make it easier to fall and stay asleep.

Extracts and tea are both common forms of passionflower people use. Both have been used in research settings, so choosing between them is a matter of preference. While research into this supplement shows potential benefits for anxiety and insomnia, there is no conclusive proof of its efficacy.

There is little research into its safety. However, daily doses of up to 800 milligrams have been used safely in studies lasting as long as two months. Side effects are usually mild and may include drowsiness, confusion, and uncoordinated movements. Pregnant women should not use passionflower, as it can induce uterine contractions. There is limited research into its safety while breastfeeding.

- Hops

In addition to being the main flavoring in beer, the flowers of the hops plant are used by some people as a natural sleep aid. Like most natural supplements, the benefits of hops have not been researched enough to definitively state whether it might help people sleep better. However, there is preliminary evidence that hops supplements can help stabilize circadian rhythms and lessen the symptoms of shift work disorder. Dried hops flowers contain the acids humulone and lupulone, and their relationship with the body's GABA receptors may be part of the reason for hops' effects.

Hops is often combined with other natural sleep aids such as valerian. It can be taken as non-alcoholic beer or in dried form as a tea or dry extract. Different studies have used all three methods, and there is no evidence in favor of one form over another.

It is likely safe to consume hops in the form of non-alcoholic beer or tea, though supplemental use is only considered possibly safe due to the lack of research. Hops also has more potential side effects than some other natural sleep aids. Because it has weak effects similar to estrogen, hops can cause changes to the menstrual cycle and is not recommended for people who are pregnant or breastfeeding, or who have hormone-sensitive cancers or other conditions. Hops can also worsen depression. However, for most people, side effects are mild and may include dizziness or sleepiness.

- Cannabidiol (CBD)

CBD is a chemical known as a cannabinoid that is present in the cannabis plant. Cannabis has over 100 cannabinoids, and CBD is much different than the psychoactive delta-9-tetrahydrocannabinol (THC) cannabinoid. Most CBD is derived from hemp, which does not contain enough THC to be psychoactive.

Research into CBD has previously been limited due to cannabis regulations, but there are indications that it might help some people sleep better. To begin with, it appears to reduce the anxious symptoms of a broad spectrum of mental health conditions. It also seems that the body's own cannabinoid system affects how we sleep, making CBD more likely to have benefits. There has been some evidence that CBD can aid some sleep disorders and reduce excessive daytime sleepiness, but research is currently inconclusive.

Although CBD has been legal federally since 2018, it is not supposed to be sold as a dietary supplement. It is, however, widely available in forms such as tinctures, gummies, and oils. Because of this lack of regulatory oversight, one study found that 26% of CBD products had less CBD than they claimed, while 43% had much more. CBD appears to be largely safe with minor side effects such as tiredness, diarrhea, and changes to weight or appetite. However, its safety is unknown for people who are pregnant or breastfeeding CBD may interact with medications and adversely impact certain health conditions.

- Tart Cherry Juice

Juice from the tart cherry, also known as the sour cherry, appears to raise melatonin levels and increase the availability of tryptophan, an amino acid that may play a role in helping people fall asleep. These are promising findings, and tart cherry juice may improve sleep quality and make it easier to fall asleep. However, some studies indicate that the effect on insomnia is not as strong as established treatments like cognitive-behavioral therapy.

Studies on the health benefits of tart cherries have had participants consume the equivalent of up to 270 cherries a day, but there is no specific research into their safety. The juice, which can be very sour, is usually diluted in a small amount of water before drinking.

- Magnesium

Magnesium is a mineral naturally present in food and often added to processed foods. It is used throughout the body and is present in bones, soft tissue, and blood. Older adults are more at risk for magnesium deficiency, and one of the mineral's many roles is sleep regulation. Some research suggests that supplemental magnesium may help reduce insomnia in older adults, either when used alone or with melatonin and zinc. It may also reduce excessive daytime sleepiness in adults.

Since high levels of magnesium are available in foods

like pumpkin seeds, it is easy to supplement by eating more magnesium-rich foods. Magnesium supplements are also available in pills and tablets, including multivitamins. Magnesium aspartate, magnesium citrate, magnesium lactate, and magnesium chloride are the easiest for the body to absorb.

While magnesium is usually safe at ordinary dietary levels since the kidneys filter it out, high dosages can cause side effects like diarrhea, nausea, and abdominal cramping. Magnesium also interacts with some medication and other supplements, and very large dosages can lead to significant heart abnormalities including low blood pressure or hypotension, irregular heartbeat, and cardiac arrest.

- GABA

Gamma-aminobutyric acid (GABA) is an amino acid and neurotransmitter that plays a vital role in regulating nervous system activity. In addition to being made by the body and present in food like tea and tomatoes, GABA is available in supplement form. While it was previously believed that GABA taken orally could not pass the blood-brain barrier and was therefore not useful to the body, there is now some evidence to the contrary

Small trials of supplemental GABA have shown that it can reduce stress and may help people fall asleep more easily. It is not currently known whether GABA's effects on sleep might be due to stress reduction or another mechanism.

GABA naturally occurs in the body and in food, but there is little research into whether it is safe to take as a supplement. However, most studies have shown no adverse reactions. GABA is available in pills and may be derived from natural or synthetic sources. Research is still ongoing as to whether synthetic GABA is as effective as GABA derived from a natural source.

- Glycine

Like GABA, glycine is an amino acid and neurotransmitter made by the body and available in some foods. Glycine appears to affect sleep and pass the blood-brain barrier. Studies show that glycine appears to improve sleep quality, potentially by lowering body temperature. Taking glycine before bed may also help reduce the negative effects of insufficient sleep, which may be due to improved sleep quality or another mechanism.

Supplemental glycine is available in capsule or powder form, and there is limited knowledge about what form might be most beneficial. While glycine is part of our diet, its safety is unknown when taken in the quantities usually found in supplements.

Are Natural Sleep Aids Safe?

Natural sleep aids are not universally safe or unsafe. Sold over the counter or online, natural sleep aids do not go through the same testing and review process as prescription medicines.

In general, there is a lack of high-quality research about the effectiveness and safety of most natural sleep aids. As a result, many questions about natural sleep remedies remain unresolved. There are special considerations to keep in mind when evaluating the safety of natural sleep aids.

Adults

Many natural sleep remedies, when taken in the proper dosage by healthy adults, have few side effects. But this does not mean that all natural sleep aids are safe.

As a precaution, adults should talk with their doctor or pharmacist before taking a natural sleep aid. Adults should also stop taking natural sleep aids if they notice any abnormal health changes or side effects.

Children

Some natural sleep aids may be safe for use in children, though sleep hygiene should be encouraged before sleep aids are considered. In many cases, there is insufficient research in children to confidently evaluate the safety or efficacy of natural sleep aids.

For certain natural sleep aids, such as melatonin, short-term use is generally considered to be safe for most children, but there is limited data about long-term use.

To make sure that any medication or sleep aid does not affect their child's health and development, parents should take precautions when considering natural sleep aids for their children, including:

- Talking with their pediatrician first
- Ensuring that the dosage is meant for children and not adults
- Paying attention to the label and list of ingredients
- Looking for high-quality products that are tested by third parties to reduce the risk of tainted or mislabeled supplements

Pregnant or Breastfeeding

People who are pregnant or breastfeeding should use caution with natural sleep aids. Many ingredients have not gone through rigorous testing in people who are pregnant or breastfeeding, so little is known about potential effects on their child.

Although some products may be safe, the best approach for those who are pregnant or breastfeeding is to consult with their doctor prior to taking natural sleep aids.

Should You Talk to a Doctor Before Taking a Natural Sleep Aid?

It is advisable to talk with a doctor before starting to use any natural sleep aid. Even though these products are available without a prescription, your doctor may be able to help in several ways:

- Reviewing your other medications and the potential for interactions between them and a natural sleep aid
- Addressing your health history and the likelihood of adverse reactions from natural sleep aids
- Understanding your sleeping problems and evaluating if they may be caused by an underlying sleep disorder that can be resolved with a more specific form of treatment
- Discussing the potential benefits and risks of specific types of natural sleep aids
- Offering suggestions about dosage or timing for taking natural sleep aids
- Providing guidance about how to know whether a natural sleep aid is working or causing side-effects

Cognitive Behavioral Therapy for Insomnia (CBT-I)

Cognitive behavioral therapy for insomnia (CBT-I or CBTI) is a short, structured, and evidence-based way to deal with the frustrating symptoms of insomnia.

How it Works

CBT-I tries to figure out how the way we think, what we do, and how we sleep are all linked. During treatment, a trained CBT-I provider helps figure out what thoughts, feelings, and actions are causing the insomnia symptoms.

Thoughts and feelings about sleep are looked at and tested to see if they are true. Behaviors are also looked at to see if they help people get to sleep. Then, a provider will clear up or reframe any misunderstandings or problems in a way that makes it easier to sleep.

Most treatments take between 6 and 8 sessions. The length can vary depending on what a person needs. When given by a primary care doctor, treatment can be as short as two visits.

People often call CBT-I a "multicomponent treatment" because it uses more than one method. Sessions can have educational, cognitive, and behavioral parts.

Cognitive interventions include "cognitive restructuring," which tries to change wrong or harmful ideas about sleep.

Behavior changes can include relaxation training, controlling stimuli, and limiting sleep. All these help people relax and get into good sleep habits.

At the heart of CBT-I is giving information about how thoughts, feelings, behaviors, and sleep are connected. The order and flow of each part can change based on how the provider works and what each person needs. Here are some CBT-I techniques that are often used:

Cognitive Restructuring

People with insomnia may have wrong or dysfunctional thoughts about sleep, which can make them do things that make it harder to sleep. This reinforces the wrong or dysfunctional thoughts.

For example, having trouble sleeping before can make it hard to fall asleep again. This worry might make you stay in bed for too long to try to sleep. Both stress and spending too much time in bed can make it harder to fall asleep and stay asleep. This can turn into a frustrating nightly pattern that can be hard to break.

Cognitive restructuring starts to break this cycle by identifying, challenging, and changing the thoughts and beliefs that lead to insomnia. During treatment, common thoughts and beliefs that may be addressed include anxiety about past episodes of insomnia, having unrealistic expectations about sleep time and quality, and worrying about being tired during the day or other effects of not getting enough sleep.

With the help of a trained provider who can help evaluate them more objectively, inaccurate thoughts can be found, challenged, and changed. Homework is often given so that students can practice these skills when they are not in class.

Stimulus Control

People who can't sleep start to dread going to bed because they associate it with being awake and frustrated. They may also think of their bedroom as a place where they do things that make it hard to sleep, like eat, watch TV, or use a cell phone or computer. Stimulus control tries to change how these things are linked.

During treatment, the bed is only used for sleeping and making love. Clients are told to get out of bed if they can't fall asleep or if they've been awake for more than 10 minutes. They should only go back to bed when they're tired again. Clients are told to set their alarms for the same time every morning and not to nap during the day.

Sleep Restriction and Compression

People with insomnia often lie awake in bed for too long. Sleep restriction limits how long a person can stay in bed so that they can get back on a regular sleep schedule.

This technique is meant to make you want to sleep more and can temporarily make you feel more tired during the day. It is not recommended for people with health problems like bipolar disorder and seizures that can get worse when they don't get enough sleep.

Using a sleep diary, the first step in sleep restriction is to figure out how long a typical night of sleep is. The amount of time in bed is then changed by this amount plus 30 minutes. For example, if a person wants to sleep 8 hours a night but only gets 5, they should change their bedtime so that they sleep for 5 hours and 30 minutes. Once a person spends most of their time in bed sleeping, they can start slowly extending the amount of time they spend there.

Sleep compression is a slightly different method that is often used with older people because it is gentler. Instead of immediately cutting down the amount of time they spend in bed to the amount of sleep they get on an average night, the time they spend in bed is gradually cut down until it is close to the amount of time they spend sleeping.

Relaxation Training

Relaxation techniques can help ease the stress and racing thoughts that come with lying awake in bed. These methods can boost the body's natural ability to calm down. This is good for both the body and the mind.

The best ways to relax are those that are easy to fit into a person's daily life. Here are a few CBT-I techniques that are often used to help people relax:

Breathing exercises: CBT-I can teach many different breathing exercises. Most of these exercises have you take slow, deep breaths. Research has shown that focused breathing can slow down your heart rate and breathing, as well as make you feel less anxious, angry, and sad.

Progressive Muscle Relaxation (PMR): PMR is a method in which different muscle groups are tense and then relaxed. These techniques can be used with guided imagery or breathing exercises.

Autogenic training is a way to focus on different parts of the body and pay attention to certain feelings. A person can pay attention to feelings like weight, warmth, or relaxation.

Biofeedback is a technique that uses technology to help keep track of things like brain waves, heart rate, breathing, and body temperature. People may be able to learn to have more control over these processes if they use the information that electronic devices give them.

Guided or self-hypnosis can help people who have trouble sleeping by teaching them how to relax when given a verbal or non-verbal cue.

Meditation has many benefits, such as lowering stress and anxiety and making it easier to relax. Meditation can also be done through practices like yoga and tai chi that combine focused attention with movement.

Psychoeducation

A core part of CBT-I is teaching clients how important good sleep hygiene is. Good sleep hygiene means doing more things that help you sleep and lessening or getting rid of things that make it hard to sleep.

Some of the things that might be talked about are how diet, exercise, and the place you sleep affect your ability to fall asleep and stay asleep.

Homework

CBT-I is a group process, and practicing the skills you learn in sessions is important. A common part of treatment is giving the patient homework. Between sessions, you might have to do things like keep a sleep diary, practice questioning automatic thoughts or beliefs when they come up and improve your sleep hygiene.

Is CBT-I helpful?

When these techniques are used together as part of CBT-I with multiple components, between 70% and 80% of people with primary insomnia feel better. It takes less time to fall asleep, you sleep longer, and you wake up less often during sleep. Results tend to stay the same over time.

For some people, CBT-I works better than medications. This treatment has also been shown to work for people who are more likely than others to have trouble sleeping, such as pregnant women.

CBT-I is thought to help with many kinds of insomnia. It may even help people with short-term insomnia. This means that CBT-I may be useful for treating insomnia symptoms even if they don't meet the criteria for chronic insomnia.

Even though this treatment for insomnia has been shown to be very effective, it doesn't always work right away. It can take time to learn and use the skills that are taught in therapy. Some methods, like controlling what you do before bed and getting less sleep, can help you change your sleep habits slowly. Some people find it helpful to keep track of their progress over time so they can see small improvements that can encourage them to keep going with treatment.

If CBT-I alone doesn't help with insomnia symptoms, the American College of Physicians suggests talking to a doctor about the risks and benefits of taking sleep medications along with CBT-I.

Does CBT-I Have Risks?

For CBT-I to work, you need to be willing to face your negative thoughts and actions. Even though the risks of treatment are likely to be low, it may sometimes be painful. Talking about painful memories, thoughts, and feelings can be hard and may cause stress and discomfort in the short term.

Working with a trained CBT-I professional can help reduce the risks of this treatment because they know how to give support and tools to deal with temporary problems or setbacks.

Who Gives CBT-I?

CBT-I is usually given by a doctor, counselor, therapist, or psychiatrist who has been trained to do so. Professional groups like the Society of Behavioral Sleep Medicine and the American Board of Sleep Medicine can help you find CBT-I practitioners.

There aren't enough CBT-I professionals to meet the demand right now because so many people need this treatment. Researchers have come up with new ways to offer CBT-I, like digital, group, and self-help formats.

Digital CBT-I

Several digital CBT-I (sometimes called dCBT-I or dCBT) apps have been made to keep up with this trend, lower the cost of treatment, and give more people access to the benefits of CBT-I. The Department of Veterans Affairs has its own app called CBT-I Coach. It can be used by both veterans and people who are not veterans.

Different online resources and smartphone apps that offer dCBT-I have different purposes and require different amounts of help from the provider. Some resources just help people while they work with a trained CBT-I provider in person, while others are fully automated and don't need any help from a clinician. Other resources and apps are a mix of the two, letting people work through a pre-set program and have regular feedback sessions with a professional through e-mail or the phone.

Digital CBT-I works well to treat insomnia in kids, teens, and adults.

Even though only a few studies have directly compared dCBT-I and face-to-face approaches, it seems that both help people with insomnia feel better.

CHAPTER 4: GUT HEALTH

Poor gut health is also associated with low GABA levels and high glutamate levels, among other concerns. Aside from probiotics, there is much that can be done to improve your gut health and, thus, reduce stress and anxiety and improve mood and energy.

"Gut": What Is It?

Everyone has heard about the significance of gut health and gut health, but what exactly is the "gut"? Although some would argue that the whole digestive tract—from ingestion to excretion—is the "gut," the majority of the actual action takes place after the material has been broken down and exited the stomach.

Indeed, the stomach plays a crucial role in the process, but the intestinal system comes to mind when considering the gut, mostly the small intestine, which is responsible for about 90% of nutritional absorption. Many food intolerances also originate in the small intestine. About 70% of people are lactose intolerant, and after consuming a dairy product, they may have diarrhea, nausea, bloating, gas, or stomach discomfort for 30 to 2 hours.

Individuals who are lactose intolerant have trouble digesting milk products because they do not create enough lactase, an enzyme that aids in the breakdown of milk sugars. After ingesting dairy products, undigested lactose remains in the gut and ferments, causing the symptoms that many individuals have.

Therefore, the small intestine is really the major location of the often reported "stomach ache" or "upset stomach"! The large intestine, also known as the colon, is the primary location for the microbiome—the community of beneficial bacteria—while the small intestine is responsible for nutrition absorption and a host of other processes. In actuality, the intestinal tract contains the whole "gut" that we are all talking about.

Gut Microbiome and Flora

The majority of readers have almost certainly heard the terms "gut flora" and/or "microbiome," but what exactly is the microbiome? And what's meant by gut flora?

All of the bacteria, viruses, fungus, and other tiny creatures that reside in your intestines are together referred to as the microbiome. We refer to those same microorganisms as the gut flora. I know it seems scary, because fungus and bacteria are nasty, right? Not all of them, however. Beneficial microorganisms are essential to bodily processes. Your general health is really primarily dependent on maintaining a healthy gut flora.

The microbiome serves a wide range of purposes. Maintaining a healthy gut flora facilitates digestion by assisting the body in breaking down certain meals that the stomach and small intestine are unable to process. Additionally, gut flora contributes significantly to the immune system by acting as a barrier, stopping the development of dangerous bacteria, and assisting in the synthesis of vitamins B and K.

Studies have even connected the gut-brain axis's health and function to the microbiome. Experts now refer to this microbiota as an "organ," given its primary role in the body's regular operation and the many tasks it performs. Nonetheless, because the microbiome is not innate, it is regarded as an "acquired organ," beginning at birth and changing throughout the course of a person's life.

The total weight of microbiota may reach up to 2 kg (4 lbs). The cecum is a little area of the big intestine that is home to a significant population of these bacteria. The region where the small intestine joins the large intestine, known as the cecum, is pouch-like and located close to the appendix.

Microbes may also be found in the stomach, esophagus, and small intestine, but in much lesser quantities. Healthy intestinal walls will be able to host more of that ideal microbiota than an unhealthy intestinal wall since these microorganisms reside in the mucosal lining of the intestinal wall. In order to increase the amount of good gut flora, several diets and supplements may also be beneficial. These supplements are often probiotics.

Probiotics

For those who have visited health stores, attended natural product exhibits, or read up on health trends, it is evident that prebiotics and probiotics are becoming more and more popular. In 2012 alone, there were about 3 million more persons in the US using probiotic or prebiotic supplements than there were in 2007, a four-fold increase in the usage of these supplements. These figures have only gone up in the last several years. However, you may want to grasp what the distinction is between probiotics and prebiotics before getting too technical.

In actuality, prebiotics and probiotics vary greatly. Dietary components like fiber are referred to as prebiotics because they aid in the development of beneficial bacteria in the stomach. These consist of flaxseeds, apples, oats, garlic, asparagus, and bananas, among other things.

Probiotics, on the other hand, are real, live microorganisms that are said to provide several health advantages, including assistance for the digestive system. Live culture yogurts, fermented meals and drinks, nutritional supplements, and even non-oral items like skin lotions are all marketed as probiotic goods.

Though some people may find the concept of purposefully ingesting germs and microbes unusual or unsettling, the advantages of probiotics have made this notion more popular among the general population. Probiotic bacteria aid in vitamin production, aid in food digestion, and eliminate pathogenic microbes. Furthermore, a large number of the microbes included in probiotic supplements are identical to or comparable to those that our bodies naturally contain in order to carry out these tasks.

Recognize that not all probiotics are created equal while reading about how to choose one. Probiotics include a wide variety of microorganisms that, while belonging to the same family of bacteria, have distinct roles in the body.

For instance, the most prevalent are from the Bifidobacterium and Lactobacillus families. Numerous bacterial species from each of these two groups' respective families are included. If one strain of Lactobacillus bacteria is shown to be protective against a disease, it is not a given that another strain would be as effective. When adding new bacteria to their bodies, those with compromised immune systems or major medical conditions should exercise caution. Apart from probiotics, several dietary supplements may also assist to enhance the intestinal environment and increase the hospitality of beneficial bacteria. In any case, it is essential to speak with a doctor before starting a new nutritional supplement.

Leaky Gut

Increased intestinal permeability, a condition where toxins and germs may seep past the intestinal wall and into the circulation, is essentially what is meant to be understood when one has a leaky gut.

Our food is broken down by the digestive system into usable nutrients, which are then transferred to the bloodstream and distributed throughout the body as required. Furthermore, the digestive system functions as a physical gatekeeper, permitting only useful substances to pass through.

Tight junctions are the name for these gatekeepers. Tiny gaps called tight junctions exist throughout the intestinal wall. They let water and nutrients pass through while blocking the passage of germs and poisons into the circulation. The so-called leaky gut syndrome results from these tight connections becoming loose, which essentially makes the gut wall more permeable to both dangerous bacteria and toxins as well as helpful chemicals. Inadequate circulatory circulation of germs and toxins leads to hyperactive immune response and systemic inflammation. This subsequently causes gastrointestinal bloating, excessive wind, poor digestion, tiredness, underproductivity, and even skin issues—symptoms of a leaky gut.

Many people are still curious about the etiology of leaky gut. Although research on leaky gut syndrome is ongoing, zonulin is assumed to be partially or maybe entirely to blame. The gut may become more permeable if this protein is activated by intestinal bacteria that have seeped out of it. Numerous factors may cause zonulin activity, such as consuming a diet heavy in sugar, using non-steroidal anti-inflammatory medicines (like ibuprofen) for an extended period of time, stress, inflammation, and routinely consuming excessive amounts of alcohol.

We are hearing more about the illness these days as researchers gain better understanding of the gut and its function in immune system and general health. More people are taking responsibility for their own health, reading up on topics, and learning about ailments like leaky guts. We then desire to take action to mend our own intestines after realizing that's maybe what we've had all along. Chronic fatigue syndrome, fibromyalgia, diabetes, Crohn's disease, and a few food allergies have all been linked to leaky gut syndrome. Making every effort to stop and fix a leaky gut may help shield us against long-term illnesses.

Absorption

Absorption is a critical component of gut health that is often disregarded. In the nutrition and supplement sectors, this phrase is often used. However, how many people really get it? The small intestine, which is the primary location of nutrition absorption, is where it all begins. These nutrients need to cross the intestinal lumen, enter the mucosal cells that line the digestive system, and finally enter the circulation in order to be absorbed. Several processes are involved in this, and they vary depending on the kind of nutrient that is flowing through.

First is diffusion. Simply said, this is the movement of molecules from a high concentration location to a lower concentration area. Molecules may effortlessly pass the cell membrane on their own when simple diffusion is occurring.

Osmosis, or the dispersion of water, comes next. Then came enhanced diffusion, in which the nutrient enters the circulation without the requirement for a carrier or transport molecule. The transportation mentioned above are all passive and don't need energy to operate. Additionally, there is active transport, which requires a carrier molecule in addition to energy to be absorbed. In contrast to straightforward passive diffusion, this kind of transport may carry materials from a lower concentration into a greater concentration.

Even though the body naturally absorbs nutrients, having a sick stomach might reduce the amount of nutrients that are really absorbed and used by the body. Certain supplements for gut health may assist to improve this absorption, which will raise the vitamins, proteins, and other vital components in our meals' bioavailability.

Bioavailability

Simply said, bioavailability is the amount of a nutrient that the body can absorb and utilize. The vitamins and minerals we ingest have widely differing levels of bioavailability. Almost all of the sodium we consume is absorbed by the body because some minerals, like sodium, are absorbed at a very high percentage. In contrast, just around 25% of what we consume is usually absorbed when it comes to calcium. Iron has much less, at 5%.

Generally speaking, the body absorbs animal goods more readily than plant ones. This is due to the fact that plants include compounds like fiber, phytates, tannins, and oxalates that bind minerals in the digestive system and limit absorption. Regrettably, the body would benefit from these plant-based diets' increased bioavailability since they include a lot of nutrients.

For instance, turmeric is well known for its antioxidant and anti-inflammatory qualities, yet its bioavailability is often poor. Many firms incorporate compounds that promote absorption to assist the increase of the bioavailability of curcumin, the main chemical in turmeric, so that lesser quantities taken will have a bigger impact. This allows consumers to actually benefit from turmeric's anti-inflammatory properties. Once again, it is critical to consider the impact those gut-enhancing substances have on absorption. Do they swell up to force nutrients through? Or instead, do they collaborate with the stomach to stimulate natural transporters and repair the lining?

A Diet for Gut Health

Our whole health is directly impacted by the condition of our stomach. Immune system strength, mood, and food digestion are all influenced by the integrity of our gut; difficulties with food digestion brought on by a compromised gut may result in inadequate nutrition and even disease.

Our microbiome, a vital collection of billions of bacteria, fungi, and viruses, lives in our stomach. These microbes, also known as "good bacteria," support the proper function of our digestive tract. Furthermore, the microbiome in our stomach affects our skin, immune system, emotional and physical well-being, and risk of contracting illnesses like cancer. Take care of our microbiome, and it will take care of us. Our gut health and microbiota are influenced by the foods we consume, so what should we eat more of and less of to keep our guts healthy?

Pickles, kimchi, sauerkraut, kombucha, yogurt, and kefir are examples of fermented foods and beverages that are excellent for the digestive system. They have probiotic bacteria, which aid in keeping the harmful bacteria out of our digestive tract and helping the healthy bacteria populate it. A particular kind of fiber known as prebiotics is what the microbes in our microbiome love to eat. Prebiotic fibers include inulin, which is found in foods like garlic, onions, and leeks. Good-for-you meals also aid in the absorption of water by the colon, facilitating the easy movement of waste products and food throughout the whole length of the intestines. Fruits, vegetables, legumes, and whole grains fall within this category.

Food that May Impair Gut Health

The adage that fresh veggies and whole grains are healthy while processed red meats, sweets, and saturated fats are unhealthy has a basis that goes beyond heart health and weight control. Sugary, salty, and high-fat diets are terrible for the intestines. As much as possible, steer clear of processed meats, baked goods, desserts, chips, fried meals, and fast food if you want to strengthen the health of your digestive system. Store them as seldom sweets.

And trust your instincts. Many individuals have dietary intolerances to certain proteins, like gluten, or sugars, such lactose, which is present in dairy products. You should stay away from these foods if they make you feel bloated, gassy, or uncomfortable after eating them. You may be intolerant to them. A sick stomach will physically talk to you. As it attempts to process the food you consume, it will gurgle and create sounds that are beyond your control. Along with gas and bloating, you could also feel gastrointestinal aches that go throughout your body. Along with regular weight gain or loss, you could also have diarrhea or constipation.

Digestion is not the only symptom of a sick gut. Because of the gut-brain link, having a bad stomach may cause mood changes, depression, difficulty concentrating, and even skin conditions like eczema. Also, you might have difficulty getting a decent night's sleep, which would leave you feeling drained and agitated all the time. For many people, these symptoms are frequent and daily occurrences, and they are often attributed to other factors like stress or just having a busy life. If this describes you, it may be time to listen to your body and your nutrition. You may regain control over your health and find the correct path to gut health by learning to listen to your body's cues.

What is your gut telling you?

CHAPTER 5: STRESS

Of course, everybody experiences stress, but when stress becomes overwhelming or too persistent then it can have a wide range of negative consequences, including a negative impact on mental health, in part by decreasing GABA signaling and increasing glutamate levels.

Between 70 and 80 percent of all diseases and ailments are stress-related, and lifestyle diseases are the primary cause of mortality. However, we do not need statistics to tell us that when we neglect ourselves, we feel anxious, fatigued, and creatively drained. Below is a list of one hundred strategies to alleviate tension.

Environmental Techniques

The first area to investigate for stress-reduction strategies is your immediate environment.

What are you able to see, sense, hear, feel, and taste? What causes you to lower your shoulders and exclaim "Ahhhh"? Consider methods to add elegance to your surroundings. Here are a few items to help you get started:

1. Have fun just being
2. Light a scented candle
3. Aromatherapy
4. Baking
5. Adjust lighting

6. Plant flowers
7. Buy yourself a bouquet.
8. Create a collection of things you love
9. Put up a bird feeder and observe the birds
10. Read in the sunshine
11. Sip a heated or cold drink
12. Snuggle up with a book under a comforter.

Cognitive Techniques

The second domain to target when reducing stress is how you process and interpret information. Your emotional response is determined by your mental interpretations, so ruminating on problems, imagining the worst-case scenario, and berating yourself for errors will all increase your tension levels. Alternately, allowing yourself to make blunders and moving on, considering the best-case scenario, and interpreting errors as learning opportunities will reduce stress.

Here are some cognitive stress-reduction strategies:
13. Reframe the issue
14. Be positive
15. Meditate on positive words
17. Practice positive affirmations
18. Maintain reasonable expectations
19. Visualize the desired outcome.
20. Display affirmations on a mirror

21. Solve a riddle or game

Innovative Techniques

Creativity is an excellent method for transforming tension into loveliness. Utilize the arts to both unwind and process your difficulties. Process is more essential than product. These are some inventive techniques for relieving stress:

22. Write in a journal

23. Write a letter

24. Paint

25. Draw

26. Spend an afternoon photographing

27.. Create pottery/work with clay

28. Knit/Crochet/Needlework

29. Pet a pet

30. Listen to/compose relaxing music

31. Play an instrument

32. Attend a concert

33. Begin a new passion

34. Garden

Physical Techniques

Frequent physical manifestations of stress include tense muscles, apprehensive movement, and rigidity. Stretching, aerobic exercise, and rhythmic motion can be utilized to relieve tension. Care for your body by making nutritious dietary choices. Try the following to physically reduce stress:

35. Dance

36. Ride a Bike
37. Run
38. Walk/hike in nature
39. Walk the dog
40. Train for a walking/marathon fundraiser
41. Swim.
42. Snorkel.
43. Get a massage.
44. Give yourself a foot massage
45. Soak your feet in warm water
46. Enjoy a steamy bubble bath
47. Take a yoga class
48. Practice t'ai chi
49. Do progressive muscular relaxation
50. Frequently practice deep breathing
51. Watch an exercise video
52. Eat a healthy diet
53. Drink water

Humorous Techniques
55. See a comedy film.
56. View a humorous sitcom
57. Read a comic book.
58. Laugh out loud
59. Tell a friend a joke
60. Laugh with a friend

Spiritual Techniques

We are holistic creatures, and our spiritual nature can also help alleviate tension. Try the following spiritual preventive measures for stress:

61. Pray

62. Meditate

63. Practice gratitude

64. Take part in a religious service

65. Sing joyful songs/hymns

66. Seek opportunities to serve others

Management Techniques

Due to procrastination, disorganization, and lack of attention to the smallest of details, some tension is created or exacerbated. By organizing your time, money, plans, and debris, you can alter your mood in as little as 15 minutes. Some management strategies include:

67. Time management

68. task prioritization

69. Delegate

70. Create and adhere to a budget

71. Solve one problem

72. Clean a room

73. Organize a cabinet or closet

74. Set objectives

75. Create a life list

76. Visualize achievement

Relationship Techniques

As long as we interact with others, relational tension will exist. This is even more vital in relationships that are meaningful to us. However, just as relationships can cause tension, they can also alleviate it. Try these relationship techniques to reduce stress:

77. Cook a special meal for a loved one

78. Be politely assertive

79. Vent to a friend.

80. Meet someone for lunch/coffee.

81. Call a friend

82. Get a manicure

83. Get a haircut

84. Email a friend

85. Join a social-support group

86. Join a fitness class or group

87. Forgive an offense

88. Volunteer

89. Do something just for fun

Outdoor Techniques

Being outdoors can alter our disposition by literally giving us a new perspective. Regardless of the weather or climate, you can implement outdoor stress relief strategies for a fast or leisurely activity. The following outdoor strategies may prove useful:

90. Sit on a park bench and use the senses

91. Stroll through a zoo or aquarium

92. Star gaze

93. Spend some time boating or sailing

94. Take a scenic drive

95. Build a sandcastle

96. Build a snowman

97. Hear the crackling of a campfire

98. Have a picnic near water

99. Eat dinner out

100. Window shop

In conclusion

Now you have a list of 100 ways to reduce tension, but they will be ineffective if they remain on paper. Choose at least one and use it immediately. Create a plan (management strategy) to implement one stress management technique per day for the next week. Combining a physical and external strategy, take a vigorous 10-minute walk outside.

CHAPTER 6: DIET

Throughout this book, food has been a common topic, but now we will take a more in-depth look at which foods promote healthy digestion and which foods might harm it. Fluctuations in blood sugar from eating too many refined or added sugars can reduce GABA and increase glutamate. In addition to maintaining stable blood sugar levels, healthy eating also fosters good gut health, provides your body and brain with sufficient vitamins, minerals, and amino acids, and offers a wide variety of other benefits in preventing disease and encouraging good health and longevity.

Gut health is a complex topic, and conflicting recommendations online can make it challenging to understand which foods are best for supporting a balance of beneficial gut bacteria.

Below you'll find a gut health grocery list with tips for how you can start shopping for foods that support healthy digestion.

For individualized advice and meal planning help to improve your gut health, consider booking a call with a registered dietitian.

Gut Health Grocery List Basics

When writing a grocery list for digestive health, the first step is understanding how different foods and eating patterns can impact the gut microbiome (all of the bacteria in your digestive system).

Your digestive tract contains trillions of bacteria, and

many factors, including food choices, can influence the types of bacteria present. When planning your grocery list for gut health, you'll want to include foods from the following categories for a nutritionally complete diet.

- Complex carbohydrates for energy and fiber.
- Protein for satiety.
- Fruits and vegetables for vitamins, minerals, antioxidants, and fiber.
- Healthy fats for satiety and vitamin absorption.
- Pantry staples and frozen goods for convenience.

What is Dysbiosis?

Dysbiosis occurs when there is a disproportionate level of harmful bacteria in your gut. It can result in gastrointestinal symptoms like bloating, upset stomach, and gas. It may also cause inflammation and impact immune function, which has been linked to an increased risk of chronic conditions like diabetes, obesity, and cancer.

Research shows that people who follow a Mediterranean diet have greater levels of health-promoting gut bacteria and a lower risk of chronic diseases. This diet consists of minimally processed foods, fruits, vegetables, legumes, healthy fats, whole grains, and limited amounts of animal products.

In addition, food sources of prebiotics and probiotics benefit gut health. Prebiotics, like onions, asparagus, and oats, act as food sources for your healthy gut bacteria to grow.

Probiotics, on the other hand, are foods or supplements that contain live active cultures (good bacteria) and are typically found in cultured or fermented foods, like yogurt, kefir, sauerkraut, and kimchi.

Foods to Include for Gut Health

When considering the foods to include or exclude from

your diet, it's important to understand that one size does not fit all. If you've been diagnosed with a specific gastrointestinal disorder, there may be a different set of dietary guidelines to help your symptoms.

For example, people with irritable bowel syndrome (IBS) may need to limit certain types of fiber, while those with celiac disease must avoid gluten. If you have chronic digestive symptoms, talk to your doctor to determine the underlying cause before making major dietary changes.

A doctor or registered dietitian can help guide your food choices to support gut health based on your medical history, symptoms, and food intolerances or allergies.

Protein

Research shows that a high intake of animal proteins, especially red meat and certain kinds of dairy, can increase harmful gut bacteria. Plant-based proteins have a protective effect and help support the growth of health-promoting bacteria in the digestive tract. Some health proteins include:

- Beans, like pinto beans, garbanzo beans, and black beans.
- Lentils, including red lentils, brown lentils, and green lentils.
- Peas, such as split peas and yellow peas.
- Soy protein, such as tofu, edamame, and tempeh.
- Poultry, like chicken and turkey.
- Fish, including salmon and tuna.
- Eggs.
- Cultured dairy, like yogurt, kefir, and probiotic cottage cheese.

Carbohydrates

Some carbohydrates contain fermentable dietary fiber, meaning bacteria can digest it in the large intestine, supporting a healthy gut microbiome. This type of fiber is primarily found in whole-grain foods.

On the other hand, refined carbohydrates and sugar can negatively impact gut health. Though gluten is commonly excluded in eating plans for gut health, research actually shows a gluten-free diet may decrease the number of healthy gut bacteria. However, it may be important for those with certain diagnoses, such as Celiac disease, to avoid gluten. Here are some healthy carbohydrates you might want to consider adding to your diet:

- Barley.
- Farro.
- Amaranth.
- Wheat, such as wheat berries, whole wheat pasta, and whole wheat bread.
- Rye.
- Brown rice.
- Oats.
- Quinoa.
- Corn.
- Potatoes.

Healthy Fats

There is evidence that a high-fat diet consisting of primarily saturated fats (common in Western diets) can negatively impact the balance of gut bacteria and increase inflammation. Therefore, focusing on monounsaturated fats and omega-3 polyunsaturated fats is best for the gut microbiome. Here are some examples of health fats:

- Extra virgin olive oil.
- Avocados and avocado oil.
- Nuts and nut butters, like peanuts, walnuts, and almonds.
- Seeds, like chia seeds, flax seeds, hemp seeds, and sunflower seeds.
- Fatty fish, like salmon, trout, and tuna.

Fruits

Fruits are rich in polyphenols, which are beneficial plant compounds naturally found in certain foods. Research has linked a higher polyphenol intake with an increase in the number of healthy gut bacteria.

Fruits also contain antioxidants, which have anti-inflammatory properties that support gut health. All fruits are a good source of fiber, and many have prebiotic fiber, which helps your good bacteria grow. These include:

- Berries, like blueberries, strawberries, and blackberries.
- Mango.
- Citrus, like oranges, grapefruit, and clementines.
- Grapes.
- Cherries.
- Papaya.
- Pineapple.
- Apricots.
- Peaches.
- Apples.
- Kiwis.

Vegetables

Like fruits, vegetables are excellent sources of gut-friendly antioxidants. Vegetables contain prebiotic fiber, which is important food for healthy gut bacteria. Pickled vegetables are a great source of probiotics, which help introduce health-promoting bacteria to your digestive tract. Here are some examples of some vegetables that support digestive health:

- Bell pepper.
- Beets.
- Cauliflower.
- Broccoli.
- Leafy greens, like spinach, romaine, and kale.
- Winter squash, including butternut squash, pumpkin, and acorn squash.
- Carrots.
- Artichoke.
- Onion.
- Asparagus.
- Brussels sprouts.
- Mushrooms.
- Pickled vegetables, including kimchi, sauerkraut, and probiotic pickles.

Pantry Staples

Consider always keeping your kitchen stocked with the following pantry staples so that you always have the basic ingredients to create a homemade meal. Then, you can supplement this list with fresh foods from the above lists, like fruits, vegetables, avocados, cultured dairy, and lean proteins.

- Dried beans and lentils.
- Frozen, unflavored fruits and vegetables.
- Olive oil.

- Grains, like farro, quinoa, and barley.
- Oats.
- Whole wheat or bean-based pasta.
- Potatoes.
- Nuts, seeds, and nut butters.
- Onions.
- Garlic.
- Pickled vegetables.
- Chicken, beef, or vegetable broth.
- Dried herbs and spices.
- Brown or wild rice.

Foods to Avoid

Conflicting information exists online, recommending people avoid foods like soy, gluten, and legumes for gut health. However, the evidence does not support eliminating these foods from a healthy person's diet to improve digestive function.

Of course, some people may have individual intolerances or conditions requiring avoidance of some of these foods.

Though dairy is often on lists of foods to avoid for gut dysfunction, the data is mixed. While a few small studies show milk may increase certain types of harmful bacteria, other evidence has found the type of fat present in dairy may benefit gut health. In addition, cultured dairy products are an important source of probiotics for many people.

Research has linked certain foods to the growth of harmful bacteria, including:

- Refined grains, like white rice and products made with white flour.
- Added sugars.
- Red meat.

- Processed meats, such as bacon, sausage, and pepperoni.
- Saturated fats, found in foods like butter and fried foods.
- Ultra-processed foods, like chips, soda, and fast food.
- Artificial sweeteners.
- Alcohol.

CHAPTER 7: EXERCISE

The good news is that exercise, which is known to improve brain health and mental ability in many ways, has been shown to raise GABA levels. Exercise may help ease some of the effects of having low GABA and high glutamate levels, as well as calm the mind.

In one study, people who had never done yoga before saw bigger changes in their mood and anxiety after a 12-week yoga intervention compared to a metabolically matched walking exercise. The amount of GABA in the thalamus rose by 13% in the participants.

After just one lesson, experienced yoga practitioners had higher levels of GABA.

In another study, yoga was compared to reading. The researchers found that people who had done yoga before had 27% more GABA in their bodies after just one lesson.

In a study on high-intensity exercise, 38 people were told to cycle (with growing intensity) until they reached or went over 80% of their maximum heart rate. After doing this, their GABA levels went up. It took 8 to 17 minutes to do.

Although GABA and glutamate work together to keep the overall amount of activity in our brains in check, having too little GABA or too much glutamate is linked to a lot of health problems. A daily yoga practice and/or high-intensity exercise routine may help with these conditions by raising the "calming chemical" in the brain.

In addition to increasing GABA, as well as a plethora

of other "feel good" chemicals, exercise has also been shown to increase serotonin levels. Since serotonin works with GABA, increasing serotonin will help your brain make better use of its GABA.

Exercise is a third way that may help raise serotonin in the brain. After a thorough look at the link between exercise and mood, it was clear that exercise has antidepressant and anxiety-reducing effects. In the UK, the National Institute for Health and Clinical Excellence, which works for the National Health Service and makes treatment recommendations based on the best evidence available, has put out a guide on how to treat depression. The guide suggests that people with mild clinical depression should be treated with different methods, like exercise, instead of antidepressants, because taking antidepressants isn't worth the risk for people with mild depression. Exercise makes people feel better, both in and out of the hospital. The effect is most consistent when people who work out regularly do aerobic exercise at a level they are used to. Some people still don't believe that exercise can help with depression, so the National Institute of Mental Health in the United States is funding a clinical trial to find out. This trial will look at the antidepressant effect of exercise and try to fix problems with internal and external validity that have limited previous research.

Several types of research show that exercise makes the serotonin in the brain work better. Post and his colleagues looked at biogenic amine metabolites in the cerebrospinal fluid (CSF) of depressed people before and after they got more active to mimic mania. Physical activity increased 5-HIAA, but it is not clear if this was because serotonin was used up faster or because CSF from higher regions, which has more 5-HIAA, was mixed with CSF from the lower back (or to a combination of both mechanisms). Still, this finding led to a lot of research on the effects of exercise on animals.

Chaouloff and his colleagues found that exercise raised the

levels of tryptophan and 5-HIAA in the ventricles of rats. Recent studies that used intracerebral dialysis have shown that exercise raises the levels of extracellular serotonin and 5-HIAA in the hippocampus, cortex, and other parts of the brain. This effect may happen through two different ways. Jacobs and Fornal looked at the research and found that motor activity makes serotonin neurons fire more often, which causes more serotonin to be released and made.

The most research on how exercise affects the amount of tryptophan available to the brain in humans is based on the idea that fatigue during exercise is linked to more tryptophan and serotonin being made in the brain. A lot of evidence shows that exercise, especially exercise that makes you tired, raises the level of plasma tryptophan and lowers the level of plasma branched chain amino acids (BCAAs), which are leucine, isoleucine, and valine. The BCAAs stop the brain from getting tryptophan. Because of the increase in plasma tryptophan and decrease in BCAA, there is a substantial increase in tryptophan availability to the brain.

Tryptophan works well as a mild sedative, which led to the idea that it might be involved in fatigue. Also, exercise causes the ratio of tryptophan to BCAAs in the blood to rise before fatigue sets in. The results of these studies show that a rise in the availability of precursors should increase serotonin synthesis in humans during and after exercise.

As with exposure to bright light, people's level of vigorous physical activity has changed a lot since they were hunters and gatherers or mostly worked in agriculture.

The decline in vigorous physical exercise and, in particular, effort-based rewards may contribute to the high rate of depression in today's society. The way exercise affects serotonin suggests that the exercise itself may be more important than the rewards it brings. If trials to see if exercise can prevent depression work, depression prevention can be added to the many other

ALEXANDER WRIGHT

benefits of exercise.

CHAPTER 8: SUPPLEMENTS

One last word on GABA supplements: Though some research concludes that GABA is not able to cross the blood-brain barrier and is therefore ineffective as a supplement, a long-standing explanation is that GABA supplements work only for those who have a compromised, or leaky, blood-brain barrier.

But new theories are coming to light. Research suggests that certain areas of the brain allow small amounts of GABA to enter. Another possibility is that GABA binds with receptors found in the peripheral nervous system, rather than those in the brain.

Taking a synthetic GABA supplement may or may not work for you. The only way to know for sure is to give it a try.

But aside from supplementing with GABA itself, there are a number of supplements that are known to increase GABA levels in the brain. Some of these include:

Taurine

Taurine is a great place to start when you want to boost GABA. Taurine is an amino acid that is found in large amounts in the brain. It works like a neurotransmitter by turning on GABA receptors. Furthermore, taurine helps the production and release of GABA.

Magnesium

Because it binds to and stimulates GABA receptors in the brain, magnesium can help reduce stress. Magnesium supplements might help if you're "tired but wired," have trouble sleeping all the time, or often get leg cramps at night.

L-theanine

L-theanine is an amino acid that is only found in black, white, green, and oolong teas. It is a very relaxing acid.

It raises the amounts of GABA, serotonin, and dopamine, which are three other important neurotransmitters that change mood.

Adaptogens, like L-theanine, are substances that relieve stress and make people better able to handle all kinds of worry. L-theanine changes mental states in a way that is similar to meditation, which is an interesting property.

The alpha brainwave state is linked to calmness and relaxation, while the beta brainwave state is linked to tension and worry. Either GABA or l-theanine will make alpha waves stronger and beta waves weaker.

It is possible to get more l-theanine by drinking tea or taking theanine tablets.

Three cups of green tea a day will not only help you relax, but it may also be good for your health in other ways.

Kava

Kava (Piper methysticum), which is also known as kava kava, was first used by people in the South Pacific to make a ritual tea that was meant to relax them.

But it is also now known to be a very effective herbal way to relieve stress. Kava works in part by raising the amount of GABA in the body.

For people with anxiety and generalized anxiety disorder (GAD), it works just as well as the prescription drugs Buspirone and Opipramol.

It also shows hope for treating ADHD because it improves brain function and makes you feel calm.

Kava can be taken as a supplement, or it can be drunk as tea, which is how it was traditionally used.

Psychobiotics

As of now, Lactobacillus brevis has been found to make the most GABA. Lactobacillus paracasei and Lactobacillus buchneri are two other top GABA makers. Lactobacillus rhamnosus raises GABA levels and makes it easier for the vagus nerve to connect the gut to the brain.

Although these bacteria already live in your gut, taking a probiotic supplement can help them grow and make more GABA.

Keep in mind that L. paracasei and L. buchneri will be harder to find than L. brevis and L. rhamnosus. You can easily find them in many probiotic products.

PharmaGABA

PharmaGABA® is a natural form made by the bacteria Lactobacillus hilgardii. Most GABA supplements are made in a lab. This good bacteria is naturally found in wine and fermented dairy products.

Two clinical studies have shown that this supplement is good for your health. It's said to bind to GABA receptors in the peripheral nervous system after being eaten, which is where the "relaxation response" happens 5 to 30 minutes after eating it.

PharmaGABA can be found in GABA products made by Swanson, Natural Factors, and Thorne.

Various Herbs

Herbs that help people relax, like valerian, skullcap, lemon balm, chamomile, and passionflower, have been used for hundreds of years to help people feel calm and sleep.

The fact that these herbal remedies have been shown to work on GABA systems in the brain is not an accident.

You can get them in the form of drinks, pills, capsules, extracts, and powders. You can also use the essential oils from these herbs to calm down and avoid worry.

Ginkgo Biloba

Ginkgo biloba, a famous memory booster, and noni fruit (Morinda citrifolia), a traditional remedy used to treat depression and anxiety, are two other traditional herbs that support GABA function.

Magnolia Bark

Magnolia bark, or Magnolia officinalis, is a useful herb that can be used in many ways. In traditional Chinese medicine, it is drunk as a tea called Saiboku-to to ease stress, nervousness, and sleeplessness. t is now sold to improve memory, ease stress, and help people sleep. It holds on to GABA receptors, which is one way it works.

Vitamin B6

The body makes the neurotransmitter GABA from glutamate, which is an excitatory neurotransmitter, and pyridoxine, which is an important cofactor.

A buildup of glutamate can also happen when you don't get enough B6. This can make anxiety, chronic pain problems, and neurodegenerative diseases worse.

Did this book help you in some way? If so, I'd love to hear about it. Honest reviews help readers find the right book for their needs. Follow **this link** *to leave a review.*

https://www.amazon.com/dp/B0CMP54ZVN

If you enjoyed this book, you may also enjoy:

The Serotonin Book: How to Maximize Serotonin Levels Naturally

The Sleep Book: How to Maximize Your Body's Ability to Sleep Naturally

The Brain Book: How to Maximize the Potential of Your Brain Naturally

Thank God for Pooping: Transform Your Mental Health by Improving Your Gut Health

Follow the author on Instagram for free book giveaways (no strings attached), free mental health information, and more:

@alexander_wright_books

For a complete list of works by this author, visit:

Badfeelingsgoaway.com

References

Professional, C. C. M. (n.d.). *Gamma-Aminobutyric Acid (GABA)*. Cleveland Clinic. https://my.clevelandclinic.org/health/articles/22857-gamma-aminobutyric-acid-gaba

Corleone, J. (2019, August 5). *A List of Foods with the Highest GABA*. LIVESTRONG.COM. https://www.livestrong.com/article/478780-a-list-of-foods-with-the-highest-gaba/

American Counseling Association. (n.d.-a). https://www.counseling.org/Resources/Library/VISTAS/2011-V-Online/Article_27.pdf

;Watson NF;Badr MS;Belenky G;Bliwise DL;Buxton OM;Buysse D;Dinges DF;Gangwisch J;Grandner MA;Kushida C;Malhotra RK;Martin JL;Patel SR;Quan SF;Tasali E; ;Twery M;Croft JB;Maher E; ;Barrett JA;Thomas SM;Heald JL; (n.d.). Recommended amount of sleep for a healthy adult: A joint consensus statement of the American Academy of Sleep Medicine and Sleep Research Society. Journal of clinical sleep medicine : JCSM : official publication of the American Academy of Sleep Medicine. Retrieved April 18, 2023, from https://pubmed.ncbi.nlm.nih.gov/25979105/

Paruthi S;Brooks LJ;D'Ambrosio C;Hall WA;Kotagal S;Lloyd RM;Malow BA;Maski K;Nichols C;Quan SF;Rosen CL;Troester MM;Wise MS; (n.d.). Consensus statement of the American Academy of Sleep Medicine on the recommended amount of sleep for Healthy Children: Methodology and discussion. Journal of clinical sleep medicine : JCSM : official publication of the American Academy of Sleep Medicine. Retrieved April 18, 2023, from https://pubmed.ncbi.nlm.nih.gov/27707447/

Oversleeping: Bad for your health? Oversleeping: Bad for Your Health? | Johns Hopkins Medicine. (2021, October 20). Retrieved April 18, 2023, from https://www.hopkinsmedicine.org/health/wellness-and-prevention/oversleeping-bad-for-your-health

U.S. Department of Health and Human Services. (n.d.). What are sleep deprivation and deficiency? National Heart Lung and Blood

Institute. Retrieved April 18, 2023, from https://www.nhlbi.nih.gov/health/sleep-deprivation#:~:text=Sleep%20deficiency%20is%20linked%20to,adults%2C%20teens%2C%20and%20children.

(n.d.). The Ultimate Guide for Gut Health | NuLiv Science. NuLiv Science. https://nulivscience.com/resources/ultimate-guide-gut-health/

Exercises That Boost Your Brain's Calming Chemical. (n.d.). https://www.mybrainfirst.com/blog/exercises-that-boost-your-brains-calming-chemical

Young, S. N. (2007, November). *How to increase serotonin in the human brain without drugs.* Journal of psychiatry & neuroscience : JPN. Retrieved March 14, 2023, from https://www.ncbi.nlm.nih.gov/pmc/articles/PMC2077351/

A. Alban, P. (2022, June 20). *GABA Supplements for Stress and Anxiety (& which work best).* Be Brain Fit. https://bebrainfit.com/gaba-supplements-stress-anxiety/

Manufactured by Amazon.ca
Acheson, AB